Classroom Advice
for New Teachers

D1521622

Classroom Advice for New Teachers

A Proactive Approach for Meeting Daily Challenges in the Profession

Jeff Julian

ROWMAN & LITTLEFIELD
Lanham • Boulder • New York • London

Published by Rowman & Littlefield
An imprint of The Rowman & Littlefield Publishing Group, Inc.
4501 Forbes Boulevard, Suite 200, Lanham, Maryland 20706
www.rowman.com

6 Tinworth Street, London SE11 5AL, United Kingdom

British Library Cataloguing in Publication Information Available

Library of Congress Cataloging-in-Publication Data Available

ISBN: 978-1-4758-4911-0 (cloth : alk. paper)
ISBN: 978-1-4758-4912-7 (electronic)

♾™ The paper used in this publication meets the minimum requirements of American National Standard for Information Sciences—Permanence of Paper for Printed Library Materials, ANSI/NISO Z39.48-1992.

Contents

Preface   ix

Acknowledgments   xiii

Introduction   xv

1   How to Recognize the Advantages of a Career in Education   1

     Lessons: Welcome to the Profession; The Teacher's Role; The Teacher's Motivation

2   How to Conduct Your Job Search   7

     Lessons: Mobility; Applying; Documents; Preparing for Your Interview; Your Demeanor During the Interview; Responding to Difficult Interview Questions; Should You Accept a Substitute Position?

3   You Won a Teaching Position! Now What?   17

     Lessons: Learn Everything You Can; Union Issues; Physical Setting of Your Classroom; When You Need Help with Supplies and Equipment

4   How to Plan Your Lessons and Keep Records   21

     Lessons: Curriculum; Character Education; Lesson Plans; Substitute Plans; Setting Up Your Gradebook; Communication; Turnaround Time and Diligence

5 How to Start the School Year   27

Lessons: Greet Your Students; Cultivate Respect; Punctuality and Behavior; Availability; Classroom Rules; Your Approach to the Rules; Structure; Student Safety and Drills; Stop Bullying Before It Starts

6 How to Present Your Material Effectively   39

Lessons: Inspiration; Keep Their Minds Working; Make It Relatable; Talent; Time on Task; How to Conduct a Discussion; Balance of Thinking and Learning Levels; Balance of Presentation; Group Projects; Public Speaking; Exceptional Student (Special) Education; English for Speakers of Other Languages; Exchange Students

7 How to Assess Student Progress   53

Lessons: Use a Variety of Assessments; Scoring; Portfolio Assessment; Standardized Tests from Your District and State; Some Things Are More Important Than School

8 How to Keep Order   63

Lessons: Motivation; Your Voice; Be Proactive Instead of Reactive; Authority; Sincerity; Planning and Pacing; Never Give an Ultimatum; Selective Enforcement; What to Do in the Event of Violence

9 How to Overcome Favoritism   73

Lessons: Empathy; Inclusion; Appreciation; Your Past Comes Back

10 How to Utilize Instructional Technology   81

Lessons: Multimedia Presentations; Web Page; Avoid Potential Problems with Technology

11 How to Handle Your Colleagues   85

Lessons: Good-Natured Professionalism; Professional Courtesy

12 How to Handle Your Administrators 91

Lessons: Meetings, In-service Days, and Assigned Tasks; More Good-Natured Professionalism; Annual Professional Performance Review; Disagreements

13 How to Handle Parents, the Community, and Public Relations 99

Lessons: Goodwill; Helicopter Parents; Enthusiasm; Field Trips; Complaining; Mandated Reporter

14 How to Handle Extracurricular Activities and Graduate Work 105

Lessons: How Many Extracurricular Activities Can You Handle?; How Much Graduate Work Can You Handle?

15 How to Overcome Negativity, Avoid Burnout, and Adapt to the Future 107

Lessons: Shared Unhappiness; Student Reference Letters; Review Your Procedures; Learn from Your Students; New Courses; Cross-Curricular Collaboration; New Ideas; Forgive Yourself and Others

Author's Note 115

Appendix A: Suggested Motivational and Review Activities 119

Appendix B: Quick Reference 123

About the Author 131

Preface

Ask students what makes a good teacher.

—ninth grader

Congratulations! If you are reading this, there is a good chance you are already a teacher, or interested in becoming one, and I consider it the greatest profession in the world. The role teachers play in the lives of students is significant, and we need to remember that it is an honor for us to do so. Your academic preparation in the field of education has been important because it provides a foundation in philosophy and subject-area content. However, this point cannot be overstated: the act of teaching occurs fundamentally in the connection you will have with each individual student. Consequently, your greatest growth as an educator will occur when you spend time in a classroom, sharpening and elevating your judgment as you perform the everyday tasks of the job and engage with students.

The good news is that many teacher-preparation programs at colleges are giving future instructors significantly more on-site experiences in public schools, and that is definitely a positive development. Even so, education students who are about to enter the teaching profession—most of whom have taken multiple courses on educational theory—are hungry for advice on exactly how to connect with students and handle the day-to-day challenges of being a successful educator. I wrote this guide to help new and aspiring teachers fill that need.

The origin of this book, and the perspective I would need in order to write it, began long ago, in the late afternoon of a dark winter day in 1985. I was a college student fulfilling an assignment by leading a discussion in my required history course. In the warmth of our third-story classroom, I experienced the electric excitement of ideas being shared and strongly held points of view being expressed, challenged, and analyzed. As I stood before my college classroom, I was surprised by the thrill I felt by conducting a simple discussion.

My professor, Dr. Joseph Gallagher, noticed my satisfaction from the act of completing his assignment and took a moment of his time, at the conclusion of the class, to encourage me to change my major from engineering to teaching. Under heavy snow and a black sky, as I left the building I saw a clear vision of my future for the first time. The entire trajectory of my life was altered. This moment of personal epiphany remains for me a testament to the influence one teacher can have over the life of a student, and I will always be grateful to him.

As much as I derived satisfaction from leading a discussion in front of college students, who were generally motivated to be there and do the work, it would be a different story altogether to effectively handle the wide spectrum of difficult situations presented to pre-K through 12 teachers every day.

My cooperating teacher during my student-teaching internship, Mr. Joseph Calarco, provided the finest example I have seen of a teacher who galvanizes the attention and engagement of his students. He employed humor, high energy, personal charisma, and inquiry-based questions to forge a strong connection with each individual in the room. Over thirty years later, the memory of his uplifting, positive command of his classroom remains a standard to which I have always aspired but doubt I have ever equaled.

Mr. Calarco also demonstrated wisdom and skill in asking me to evaluate each aspect of my performance, rather than criticizing me directly. This is a technique I believe is both effective and merciful to use with students, because it allows them to maintain their dignity as well as more deeply understand their mistakes. Many of Mr. Calarco's students would tell me that they hated school but loved Mr. Calarco and his class.

How can a new teacher achieve this kind of loyalty on the part of the students? Do not be discouraged if it does not happen right away. Continually evaluate your own performance as objectively as you can, keep the practices that work, and experiment with new techniques. When encountering my own classes for the first time, I discovered that establishing the tone and atmosphere of the room, connecting with my students, proactively avoiding problems, and effectively reacting to the ones that cannot be avoided are skills that can take years to develop.

If you would like an example, picture this: you are standing in front of a group of ninth graders as a relatively new teacher. You introduce an educational activity for the class by saying "You know what I haven't tried in a while?" to which a student replies, "A sit-up?" What do you say in response to a student comment that is disrespectful and disruptive, but undeniably humorous? Many potential options might come to mind, and your reaction to this type of comment will go a long way toward establishing the tone you create in your classroom. We will revisit this scenario later in these pages.

College and university programs for future educators are outstanding, but it is doubtful that any aspect of your education as a teacher could have prepared you for an encounter of this kind, because the range of potential challenges you are likely to face as a teacher is almost infinite. This type of situation requires a judgment call on your part that will be just one of many you will make on a daily basis as a teacher, and increasing your ability to make those decisions, as well as handle daily tasks effectively, is the reason I compiled this guide.

When you are hired for your first teaching job, you are essentially on your own. Of course, various department members, colleagues, and administrators will be willing to help you, out of empathy and basic human decency. There is nothing wrong with occasionally asking for advice or a question about school policy from a person who has experience in the system and can readily supply an answer. You may even be assigned to a mentor. It is important, though, that you use these encounters sparingly, or you will run the risk of giving the impression that you are having trouble meeting the challenges of your job. Also, remember that your administrators and colleagues are busy struggling to overcome their own challenges.

In the meantime, how do you know what course content you are responsible for covering? When you figure that out, how can you most effectively present and assess your students' mastery of that material? How do you arrange your classroom? How do you set up your gradebook? What are the rules of conduct you will establish for your classes? In addition to thinking about how to best establish a connection with your students, have you thought about how you will go about dealing with administrators, colleagues, support staff, parents, school board members, and community members? All of these practical questions are answered in this book.

Like most people in the profession, I have stumbled my way into many wrong decisions, and sometimes stumbled into right ones. In the heat of the moment, it is hard to know how to handle a difficult situation, and often it takes the perspective of a few years to recognize whether you chose the right course of action. I take every opportunity to pass on those experiences to new teachers, in the hope that they can learn from the good fortune of my successes and the misfortune of my mistakes over the course of four decades.

The idea to write this book came several years ago, on a night when I was slated to speak to a group of prospective social studies teachers at a local college. They were just days away from beginning their internship experiences and were eager for any insight into how to run a successful classroom. I thought it might be useful for them to hear advice from my students, directly from the classroom.

I had spent the last few minutes of each of my classes that day collecting quotes from my students, with the idea that they would be delivered later to the prospective teachers. That evening, when I relayed my students' quotes to the group, I noticed how eagerly they wrote down every word. I came to understand how valuable it must be to a prospective teacher to hear words of advice directly from the world in which he or she hopes to succeed. They have studied educational philosophy as well as course content but still wanted to gain knowledge and judgment concerning the daily challenges of the job.

Many of the quotes from students emphasized the importance of treating each individual with empathy and respect. One of the prospective new teachers asked if that quality can be effective in a school with socioeconomic disadvantages and sometimes dangerous behavior problems. The answer is that students on all levels of motivation, ability, and demographic conditions respond to respect, integrity, and decency, and need role models in their lives demonstrating such behavior as a way of life.

The students themselves are an underused resource for gaining insight into effective educational techniques. They have spent most of their lives dealing with a wide range of teachers, and they generally have a very accurate idea of what works and what does not work in their instruction. With that in mind, I made the decision to create this practical guide for new teachers. I have deliberately excluded research and data, and I have only briefly referenced educational theory. Instead, I have relied on my specific experiences in the classroom as well as the perspective of my students, who offer a unique and valuable point of view.

Acknowledgments

To my son, Brian, who inspired this book and continues to inspire me every day with his skillful teaching and spirit of loyalty, generosity, courage, strength, and pure, genuine goodness; my daughter, Laura, who showed me, with fearlessness and tenacity, the sweetness and beauty of this world; my wife, Sandy, who taught me the value of life and the joy of living while raising children in an oasis of love and support; my parents, Philip and Audrey, who showed me, through their fine example, the qualities of decency, strong values, and a high standard of integrity and personal conduct, along with my entire family; my sister, Michele, brother-in-law, Tim, and brother, Christopher, for their friendship and hospitality; Richard and Jennifer, who brought fresh life and joy to our family; The Untouchables, who inspire me with fellowship and good humor; my grandfather, Joseph, who taught me humility, helpfulness, and hard work; and my grandmother, Adele, whose example and advice on the importance of magnanimity, empathy, and kindness did more than anyone to shape my teaching philosophy and who had such respect for educators that she was proud of me for becoming one.

Introduction

I have organized the topics of this book into chapters, each containing student quotes and a series of specific lessons. Each lesson consists of an analysis and evaluation of actions to take and to avoid regarding the aspect of the job covered in the chapter. It is my hope that these observations offered directly from the classroom will provide new and prospective teachers with answers to the practical questions they will face when they enter their own classrooms.

Throughout the book, I have included sections called "In Practice," in which I describe an actual scenario faced by a teacher corresponding to the topic and allow the reader to choose from three possible actions on the part of the teacher in an effort to resolve the situation. This is followed by an explanation of the likely outcome of each of those options, as well as the choice and consequences actually made by the teacher.

I begin each chapter with quotes from students in italics, and throughout the lessons I have placed the main points in bold print for emphasis. The most detailed and thorough topics deal with how to begin the school year, plan lessons, present material effectively, assess student progress, and keep order, because those are the tasks that many prospective teachers feel are their most pressing concerns. At the conclusion of the book, you will find a section describing review activities that I have found to be effective throughout my career, as well as a section for quick reference of the most important ideas that you will want to remember from this guide.

At the time of this writing, most public school teachers across the United States have specific criteria on which they are judged by their administrators, called the Annual Professional Performance Review, or APPR. It uses a combination of student standardized test scores and observations by the administrators, which cover several domains of teacher performance.

The specific criteria used by your district are the most important set of standards for you to fulfill, and you need to familiarize yourself with them immediately. This book is intended as a supplement to those domains, and my intention is to cover the more practical aspects of your daily challenges and experiences.

With humility and gratitude, this is my attempt to describe the teaching profession as I have experienced it.

Thank you and best wishes to all of my students, colleagues, and administrators, past and present.

You have read the pedagogy, you have heard the theories, you have seen the data, and now it is time to stand and deliver. Here is how.

Chapter 1

How to Recognize the Advantages of a Career in Education

Be the reason that a student wants to get on the bus in the morning.

—ninth grader

If you're doing your job right, you can make a difference in a student's life.

—twelfth grader

If you love your job, students will love your class.

—ninth grader

The impact you make on your students will stay with them for the rest of their lives.

—twelfth grader

Appreciate your students.

—seventh grader

LESSON:

Welcome to the Profession

It is a tremendous privilege for you to stand in front of a group of young people and presume to explain to them what the world is like.

Whether you are studying to become a teacher, or you have completed your academic coursework and are about to encounter your students for the

1

first time, the first thing you need to do is look at your chosen profession with the proper perspective. Not many people have the privilege of influencing so many at such an impressionable time of their lives. Do not get distracted by the daily frustrations that enter your lives and your classrooms, and remember the honor that it is to play such a significant role in the lives of your students. When you remind them that you are aware of that privilege, many of those distractions and frustrations will be minimized.

LESSON:

The Teacher's Role

Always remember the honor of playing this role in the lives of your students and make sure you give an indication to them every day that you remember it.

From the start, put aside the stereotypes and negative impressions some members of the public have about teachers. For example, summer vacations are a part of the overall deal that teachers accept, along with the less-advantageous aspects of the job. It is true that most teachers are planning their classes for the following school year, continuing their education, and completing a variety of professional obligations during that time. It is also true that a large percentage of the public does not realize that teachers are doing these things and will occasionally make remarks that are negative toward the profession, especially during the summer months.

You are likely to be happier and more productive if you focus on your students and refuse to engage in controversies about the public's view of the profession.

Experience shows that the most effective way to counter that type of attitude is to accept it without argument. Quite often the harshest critics of the teaching profession have experienced legitimate frustration and disappointment with their own jobs and life choices. Unfortunately, when teachers attempt to defend themselves by pointing out the challenges and difficulties of the job and the significance of the role they play, it only tends to inspire more negativity and resentment among some members of the public. You will feel better if you try to empathize with them and put their negativity in perspective. If you are doing the job correctly, you will know the truth.

If you feel the need to respond in some way to negativity about the profession, rather than listing the difficulties and challenges you face in your teaching career, try instead the approach of gratitude and humility. You can express your gratitude for the advantages awarded to you in your teaching position, with an emphasis on being humbled by the privilege of playing such an important role in the lives of your students. Indignation, self-importance, and defensiveness on your part will frequently result in the other person increasing their resentment and searching for points with which to counteract you, while gratitude and humility almost always serve as the antidote that stops negative attacks in their tracks.

Does this response sound weak to you? Should we not have the courage to fight to defend the honor of our chosen career? That is exactly what you will accomplish. More so than any other approach, gratitude and humility have the power to neutralize any negativity aimed at schools and educators. The dignity of your behavior will also reflect well on teachers everywhere, diminishing the resentment and increasing the respect the general public has for our profession.

The factor that makes teachers important is the role they play in the lives of their students, not the act of telling others about their importance.

Above all: Stay positive in the face of criticism by showing gratitude and humility.

The salary you are likely to earn as a full-time teacher will not allow you to be wealthy, but it will probably lead you to a standard of living in the middle class. Your teaching salary will be sufficient if you live modestly, but you are not likely to match the compensation offered by other professions requiring an equivalent level of education.

Public school teachers make a trade-off. They gain significant vacation time—often coinciding with the vacation time of their own children—compared with many other professions, step increases that bring up their salaries at least a little bit during most years, the relative job security of due process, and a solid retirement system in most states.

In return, they give up the ability to win significant promotions and salary increases through extra hard work, talent, innovation, or creativity. Even though some states offer incentive pay, a young, talented, and innovative teacher will almost always receive significantly less compensation than a veteran teacher on a higher step, even if the older teacher has barely put in enough effort to avoid removal for poor performance. The overall effect is that you will be able to have a decent—but not extravagant—standard of living as a full-time teacher.

Your salary, benefits, and conditions should not be deciding factors in whether you pursue a career in education. The main consideration is whether you want to play an important role in the lives of students. If you go into teaching for the summer vacations, you will find that it is a long way to the summer.

The best teachers make their professional role into their entire way of life, as opposed to relegating teaching to the status of a means to pay bills. Make your best effort to live in the community where you teach. This will mean that your students and their parents, along with school board members, will no longer just be aspects of your working life, but they will be your neighbors and friends as well.

There is a direct benefit to this. If you live inside the district, you often have a place of importance in the community because many residents know you, along with your reputation. If you live outside the district, some members of the community can have the mistaken impression that you are a disinterested outsider coming into their town only to get a paycheck funded by taxpayers. Making your home among the people you serve gives your presence in the classroom the extra gravitas earned by being a permanent fixture in the community.

Some teachers believe that the downside to living in the district where you teach is that your behavior outside of school is closely and sometimes unfairly scrutinized. This is definitely true. However, the extra responsibility a teacher takes on by living in the district is more than rewarded by the privilege you accept by serving as a role model for so many people.

As a teacher, your words and your actions are powerful and carry a great deal of influence for your students, who are often searching for a positive view of what it can be like to be an adult. You can either embrace this privilege and live up to it, or reject it and hide from the responsibility. If you are looking to achieve the greatest possible satisfaction from your teaching career, you will accept the honor of being a role model to your students and live your life in a manner that demonstrates to your students, their parents, and the entire community that you deserve that honor.

LESSON:

The Teacher's Motivation

Make sure your students know that the reason you are a teacher is because you genuinely like working with them and want to help them.

The important word in this sentence is "genuinely," because your approach cannot be a cynical trick. If your concern for your students is not genuine, they will sense your transparent dishonesty and your relationship with them may be permanently damaged.

Keep your door open during preparation periods in order to talk with students about their successes and frustrations, academically and otherwise. You can devote a small amount of your class time for this as well. When your students are shown that you care about their progress in academics, sports, extracurricular activities, and life in general, the bond you create with them will have a positive effect on your students' motivation to perform in your class.

One way to help you bring this about is to have students complete an interest inventory at the beginning of the year, in which they list their hobbies, interests, activities, and future goals. If you keep these interests in mind, you can bring up information pertaining to those topics throughout the year to create a connection with each individual student. It gives them, correctly, the impression that you actually care about their lives, which in turn has a significantly positive impact on their motivation to learn, as well as your motivation to teach.

Just as important, your kindness and concern will serve as an example of good character that lives on in the memory of your students. A crucial point to remember: always keep your door open when meeting alone with a student in order to proactively avoid the appearance of impropriety.

Keep remembering the value of what you do, and keep searching for ways to create a bond with each student. Those positive thoughts will have to outweigh the frustrations you will face in order for you to keep moving forward with optimism, which in turn keeps the overall tone of your classroom upbeat, happy, and cooperative.

IN PRACTICE: You are a teacher who hears that one of your former students attempted to take her own life over the summer, and she is scheduled to be a student in one of your courses again during the upcoming year. She is resting comfortably at home but has expressed a strong aversion to returning to school in the fall. Her parents are worried that she might make another attempt to end her life. What should you do?

1. Ignore the situation.
2. Wait until the student returns to school before mentioning anything.
3. Send her a note expressing your excitement at having her in your class again.

Many teachers would choose the first option, because they are afraid that they might make the situation worse. Others might choose the second option, but they would most likely draw attention to the student when it's the last thing she wants when returning to school. This scenario actually took place, and the teacher chose the third option. He sent a note expressing excitement about having her as a student in his class again in the fall, along with a gift of a small stuffed animal.

A few weeks later, the teacher was approached by the student's mother, who tearfully thanked him for the note. She said that her daughter was now excited to come back to school, knowing that he would be her teacher. She ended the conversation with, "Thank you for saving my daughter's life." A person who overheard the exchange said, "In forty years at my job, no one ever said that to me."

Some careers offer generous salaries and benefits, but ours offers moments like that one. Remember that it is a privilege to be a part of this profession. Do not ever doubt the importance of what we do, and how we can positively impact the lives of so many people.

As teachers, our influence extends beyond what we know.

Chapter 2

How to Conduct Your Job Search

Stand out!

—ninth grader

Entire books have been written about the best approaches to the interview process. This advice is focused on the most practical aspects of your search for employment. Applying for multiple teaching positions can seem like a full-time job in itself, but you can minimize the amount of time you spend on it by organizing your materials efficiently.

LESSON:

Mobility

Your best chance of finding an open position is to allow for the possibility that you will have to relocate. Searching for teaching positions over a wide geographic area will give you the most choices, and in some cases, relocation may be your only option. It is important to realize, though, that teaching conditions vary considerably from state to state. Research the specific salary and benefits package offered by each district where you may pursue a position and compare it with the cost of living in the general area.

It will also be useful to investigate the teaching conditions, such as student load, number of courses, and amount of prep time, among other factors, before you decide to travel for a position. These are quality-of-life issues, and you may have to live with the conditions specified in a particular district's contract for a long time if you choose to accept a position in that district. You can find the contracts for most public school districts online.

If you are going to pursue a teaching position in another area or state, research the details carefully before you go.

Applying

Whether mobility is possible for you or not, the best way to find up-to-date openings for teaching positions is through the websites for each individual school district. At that point, you can follow their specific guidelines for applying. Some districts even keep a pool of qualified candidates on hand, and if you provide all the necessary information to them, they will contact you when they have an opening in your area of certification.

In addition, you will find websites dedicated to compiling all the teaching positions in the geographic area in which you're interested. If you find open positions in your area of certification, you can usually follow links to the human resources pages of the corresponding districts. You can then proceed with the applying, interviewing, and hiring process as established by the individual districts.

Documents

Make sure you have multiple copies of your diplomas, certificates, reference letters, and any other supporting documentation you will need. Keep all your background information compiled and stored in one easily accessible location for when you are filling out applications.

Some districts ask for a resume and cover letter, but most now require an online application process, so be sure to have all your documentation in digital form so that it can be easily uploaded. Be sure it is backed up so that it cannot be lost. Compile a portfolio to bring to your interviews, consisting of copies of your important documents, transcripts, certifications, evaluations, reference letters, as well as notes from administrators, parents, and students, and photos showing you successfully working with your classes. Be sure that everything in your portfolio is positive enough to help your cause. Otherwise, leave it out.

When preparing your resume for the first time, start with your contact information, followed by your certification and education, then teaching experience, other work experience, interests, references, and information on how to access your transcripts. Your teaching experience should be as specific as possible, including courses you've taught and procedures you have used to help students succeed. It is also helpful to include the contact information for your supervisors and administrators, but be sure to ask permission first.

When describing your interests, try to concentrate on activities that relate to your career as a teacher and ones that help you to stand out. In general, your entries on the resume should be in reverse chronological order, with more recent information first. You should only include high school information if it is very much in your favor and an indication of future success in the teaching profession. As you gain experience in the classroom, you can begin to remove older information from your resume.

While you wait for schools to respond to your interview requests, use the time to strengthen your resume by making yourself a more competitive candidate. Take the steps to gain additional subject and grade level certifications because administrators will view you as a teacher who will offer them flexibility with their scheduling. This will give you an advantage over other candidates. Continually strive to gain experience working with young people, even if you have to volunteer for literacy programs or summer camp.

Some sources tell you to make follow-up phone calls after sending an application to a school, and you should definitely verify that they received all the required materials. Beyond that point, it really will not do you any good to repeatedly bother the office staff. If a hiring committee wants to grant you an interview, you can be sure that they will be in touch.

LESSON:

Preparing for Your Interview

You have scored an interview! Now what? In order to prepare, think about the most commonly asked interview questions for teachers: "Tell us about yourself" and "What qualities can you bring to our school?" are two questions that are covered in one form or another in every interview. You should have answers prepared for each of those topics that last about a minute, including anecdotal experiences you have had that involved working with students.

As a rule, you should stay positive at all times during your interview, but your interviewer may specifically ask you to describe your greatest weakness. This is a common interview question, and it presents the problem of you having to appear to be negative in order to answer the question. The best way to handle it is to choose a mild deficiency you may have that is not your fault, followed immediately by a description of the steps you have already taken to overcome it so that the issue is no longer a deficiency.

If your interviewer asks you to describe something negative about a former teacher, principal, or coworker, do not do it. Tell them you got along very well with your coworkers and supervisors. If they ask you to describe a disagreement with a coworker or supervisor, choose a minor misunderstanding that was solved through open dialogue and ended with mutual respect.

Your Demeanor During the Interview

Dress professionally for your interview. Anything less will be viewed as a lack of respect for the people with whom you're meeting. Be sure you arrive at least fifteen minutes before the scheduled start of your interview and bring copies of your certification and other necessary documentation with you. Look each of your interviewers in the eye as you answer their questions and address them by name after the point at which you've been introduced, using "Mr." or "Ms." along with the last name. This can seem formal, but it demonstrates respect, professionalism, and attention to detail on your part.

Remember that each question is a springboard for you to demonstrate your love for the profession and your positive experiences with students. If you are in a position to interview for a teaching position, it is likely that you have taken courses on educational theory. You will almost certainly encounter at least one question on theory during your interview. Whichever philosophy you choose to convey to your interviewers as being important to you, be sure to apply those philosophies to student activities.

If you forgot most of the information in your educational theory classes, or never took them at all, here are a few examples of philosophers and how they can apply to your experiences. Piaget believed, among other things, in the concept of learning by doing. You can demonstrate your belief in that philosophy by describing how you taught a unit on fiction writing by encouraging your students to write their own stories. That also satisfies the principle behind Bloom's Taxonomy, in which synthesis—or creation—is at or near the highest level of thinking and learning.

In Bloom's Taxonomy, the other activity at the highest level of thinking and learning is evaluation, in which a person uses judgment to decide questions of quality or ethics. As such, it's a commonly required learning standard and you can use this philosophy if you have ever asked your students to write their opinions on a topic in the process of taking and defending a position.

Kagan promotes the engagement of students in the learning process. You can demonstrate that philosophy by describing a group project that required full participation by every student. Irwin believed in setting an atmosphere conducive to learning on the part of the students. You can describe how you have organized your classroom to maximize student comfort, engagement, and productivity.

Quite often, your interviewer for a teaching position will ask you if you have read a book that is outside any requirements for a high school or college course and how the book and the author affected the way you view the world. It's very important for you to prepare for this, because there are some administrators and teachers who consider a weak answer to this question to be a deal breaker for your prospective employment.

If you have not read a book other than for a high school or college requirement, do it immediately. Choose a well-known author with literary stature in order for your example to have credibility, but try to make it a book that is a lesser-known example of his or her work. That way your interviewers are less likely to suspect that you read it as an assignment.

When deciding on how the book relates to your worldview, be sure to identify a theme that is universal and philosophical. Great literature illuminates universal human experience, so if you choose a prominent and well-respected author, you should be able to draw from it a wide-ranging lesson on life. The necessity for you to find a work of literature that will prepare you for this question cannot be overstated—if you haven't accomplished this already, you need to do it immediately.

Read a book outside of school, and think about what it teaches you about life.

Another commonly asked interview question is "Where do you see yourself in five years?" The answer should always be "Right here at this school, learning and growing as a professional every day and very happy to be teaching the students of this district." You may have plans to backpack through Europe, but you will need to accept that you are going to have to make a commitment to a school that hires you.

The school wants to know that if they hire you, they will not have to go through the hiring process again in the near future, especially if they suspect that you will be using their school as a stepping-stone to a higher-rated district. It is important to reassure them by pointing out the strengths that you have noted about their school while doing your research; make sure they believe that you want to be a part of the efforts they are making on behalf of their students.

Your interviewers are likely to ask you about the subject in your area of certification, and most specifically about your background in the course material covered in the curriculum of the available position.

When asked about your background in the subject material, always concentrate on expressing what you know, not what you don't know.

For example, if the interviewers ask you about your background in biology, and you have none, respond by telling them about your success in various science classes like chemistry, physics, and earth science, along with your ability to adapt to any requirements listed in the state standards for the biology course. Your answers should always be honest in the interview, but you should never waver from bringing forth your positive qualities and avoid discussing your negative qualities or gaps in knowledge.

Be sure to show a deep interest in the subject matter in the course for which you are interviewing and a desire to help the students discover the same fascination with it that you have.

For each answer you give, try to have a corresponding anecdote about helping a student achieve success. Remember: you are deeply interested in the subject and you want to awaken the same interest on the part of your students. Throughout these descriptions, make sure you remain enthusiastic about your students, strategies, philosophies, and projects, making it apparent that you find great satisfaction in the act of teaching.

You should be sure to have several stories ready to convey to your interviewers, each involving optimism, overcoming obstacles, and student success.

If you don't think you have experiences to use, look deeper. If you have completed an internship or student teaching in any capacity, your time with students contained many small victories that can be celebrated and remembered. You need to look closely to find those victories and to effectively shape the anecdotes by choosing where to begin, which details to bring to the forefront, and which ones to eliminate. As always, keep it positive and focus on student growth and achievement.

IN PRACTICE: On a warm afternoon in August, a public school superintendent goes directly from the golf course to his office to interview a young English teacher for a position on his high school's faculty. The candidate is dressed in a professional manner, with a suit and tie. The superintendent, still wearing his casual golf outfit, remarks that the tie must be uncomfortable and asks the candidate if he expects to wear a tie every day if he were to win a teaching job in his district. How should the candidate reply?

1. "You're right—it's uncomfortable, which is why I never wear ties!"
2. "I don't usually dress like this, but I thought it would be important to show respect during my interview."
3. "I make an effort to wear a tie every day because I want to be viewed as a professional."

The first response is almost always wrong, because in effect you are saying that you almost never maintain a professional appearance. You may sometimes get away with the second option, but you're taking the chance that your interviewer doesn't expect you to dress in a more formal way on a regular basis.

In this case, the third choice happened to be the most appropriate one because the superintendent was tricking the candidate—he informed him at the conclusion of the interview that he expected all his teachers to dress professionally every day. This won't always be the case in every school in every district, but it's always safer to take the side of formality and respect over informality and a casual demeanor may be interpreted as disrespect. In this case, the candidate won the job.

During your interview, above all else, stay positive and enthusiastic at all times. Remember why you love your subject and why you love working with students and then convey that to your interviewers.

LESSON:
Responding to Difficult Interview Questions

Each interview question is asked with the intention of determining not only if you are qualified for the position, but also what it would be like to work with you, possibly for the next thirty years. Keep in mind the qualities that represent the best version of who you are and answer each question in a manner that brings across those qualities.

In order to accomplish this, make a list of the five qualities that describe you at your best. You need to be honest with yourself, and this is not the time to engage in wishful thinking. You need to put aside your negative attributes and recognize the qualities that describe the best version of yourself. If you are a creative, artistic, free spirit, do not try to pretend to be a solid, hardworking dependable person if that is not what best describes you.

Conversely, if the second description fits you, do not try to pass yourself off as the opposite. Instead, take the qualities that do represent you at your best and make the most of them. Apply that information to every interview question. This knowledge will be most useful to you during interview questions that you are not able to anticipate, and most interviews contain at least a few of these.

If you have prepared for the most commonly asked interview questions about your strengths as a professional as well as the qualities you will bring to their district if hired, but are unsure of what to do about the unusual, off-the-wall questions, the most important point to remember is to stay positive at all times, especially concerning students.

If you combine the approach of optimism and enthusiasm while keeping in mind the qualities that represent you at your best, it will be difficult for you to go too far wrong in your answer to any question.

IN PRACTICE: A candidate for a high school math position is welcomed into the superintendent's office by the superintendent himself, who tells the candidate that she has now reached the stage of the easy interview. The candidate has already successfully achieved the winning position in two of the school's previous interviews—one with the math department faculty and another with the high school principal.

During the course of the interview, the superintendent asks the candidate for an estimate of the percentage of her students who are likely to fail her class. He reminds her of the importance of rigor in any course, in order to challenge students to reach their full potential. If you hold your students to a high standard, the superintendent asks, what would be the most accurate percentage of students who will fail the course? What is the most appropriate answer?

1. "Twenty percent—I believe in challenging my students with rigorous content and holding them to a high standard."
2. "Five percent—I plan to help my students to the best of my ability, but it's inevitable that forces beyond my control will cause a small group of my students to fail despite my best efforts."
3. "Zero percent—failure is not an option in my course. I plan to do everything in my power to monitor student progress and intervene as often as necessary to guide students to success, and I'll never rest until all my students are passing my class."

The first option definitely sounds rigorous, and there is no doubt that holding students to a high standard is an admirable quality in a teacher. The second option sounds reasonable, and it is definitely true that sometimes the reasons for a student's poor performance are beyond the teacher's control.

Being a math teacher, the candidate thought carefully about the numbers involved and calculated that approximately 5 to 10 percent of her students would fail despite her best efforts to prevent it. She won the position, but weeks later the superintendent told her, in a lighthearted manner, "You're lucky you got the job. The correct answer to that question is 0 percent—we don't tolerate any failures in this school."

During your interview, make sure that any mention of students is optimistic and hopeful.

Some districts require applicants to teach a lesson to the committee in order to gain a sense of your style and demeanor. You will need to have a short lesson prepared so that you can demonstrate your ability to your interviewers. In order to do this most effectively, choose a topic that would be interesting to the committee and a procedure that calls on your interviewers to actively engage in your lesson. Sometimes a topic is chosen for you. In that case, apply that topic to your prearranged procedure that emphasizes the engagement of the committee.

An example would be to take your topic and turn it into a discussion in which you require your audience to take and defend a position. Briefly and clearly supply them with information, then ask inquiry-based, essential questions to draw out their analysis and evaluation of the issue. Make sure that you call on everyone, that your responses to the comments are positive and encouraging, and that you lead the discussion forward at an appropriate pace.

Eye contact, pitch, volume, and tone of voice, as well as movement, hand gestures, and facial expressions are all important qualities to keep in mind. Also, don't underestimate the value of smiling, and even laughing, during your presentation. Doing so as often as possible, within reason, will establish an optimistic tone that will leave a positive and uplifting impression on your interviewers. Laughing along with your questioners helps develop a bond between you, and that is definitely something you want to accomplish during any interview. You can balance the moments of levity with deeper topics on which you demonstrate seriousness of purpose in order to achieve the most effective overall impression.

After you have interviewed, follow up with a thank-you note, even if a different candidate won the job. You never know when another position will open in that district and you will want to be sure that you have not burned any bridges.

LESSON:

Should You Accept a Substitute Position?

If you have to confine your job search to a specific geographic area and you are not able to secure a full-time, permanent teaching position, you may want to consider working as a substitute teacher for one or more districts. There are advantages and disadvantages to this. The human resources page of each district should list a procedure for applying for a substitute position. If you are accepted by more than one school or even more than one district, you can work almost every school day if that's what you want.

Your experience as a substitute teacher can help you improve your classroom management techniques and give you the opportunity to develop a positive relationship with teachers and administrators, which will be an advantage if a full-time position opens in that particular school. You will have the flexibility in your schedule to be able to decide on a daily basis if you would like to work on that day, and you can travel or take time off anytime you like.

One disadvantage is that you usually will not know where you will be working on any given day or what subject you will be teaching. Sometimes the teacher for whom you are substituting will not have left adequate plans, and students tend to be less willing to accept the authority of a substitute teacher in comparison with their regular teachers. Most of the time, the pay will also be less for substitutes than for full-time, permanent teachers on the salary schedule.

With all of this in mind, it is advisable to choose a full-time, permanent position over a substitute position. This holds true even if the substitute position is long-term and in the district, school, grade level, and subject you prefer, and the full-time, permanent position is in a situation that is not ideal. The reason is that the full-time, permanent position will allow you to gain better experience, will carry more weight on your resume, and most important, will usually allow you the security of keeping the position as long as you want it so that you can take your time searching for a more advantageous situation. You may even find that you would like to stay in the position. As an added bonus, you will be accruing years of experience toward your salary schedule as well as your retirement system.

If you do choose to accept a substitute position, there are several practices you can do in order to increase the demand for your service. First, you should be aware that teachers want, more than anything else from a substitute, to know that everything went smoothly during his or her absence. Be sure to leave a note, the more positive the better, to let the teacher know that the students completed the required work.

If necessary, you can identify the students who did not do the work, but save this for extreme circumstances. The last thing a teacher wants is to discipline students and follow through with consequences for a situation that occurred when his or her students were under someone else's supervision.

Also, teachers are generally less than appreciative if the substitute tries adding to the information the students are learning in the course. You may want to show off the extent of your knowledge, but show some self-control instead and keep it limited. Never pass judgment on the teacher in front of students, or allow students to do it, even if they are making a comparison favorable to you.

Chapter 3

You Won
a Teaching Position!
Now What?

I think teachers can be influential when they build relationships with students.

—twelfth grader

Be flexible—many things will happen that you haven't planned.

—untenured teacher

Respect is earned, not given.

—twelfth grader

School is like jail.

—ninth grader

No, it's not—jail has better food.

—another ninth grader

LESSON:
Learn Everything You Can

Learn everything you can about your district, your school, and its policies as soon and as quickly as you can. The best place to start is the school's website, which should contain a teacher handbook in some form. Once you have familiarized yourself with your district's policies, you will need to begin preparing for your classes.

Find out as soon as possible which courses you'll be teaching and whether you'll have your own classroom. When you discover the courses for which you will be responsible, immediately access the curriculum and standards for those courses from both the district and the state. That process will be covered in detail during an upcoming section of this book.

LESSON:

Union Issues

Depending on your political perspective, teachers' unions are either the last line of defense against teachers losing their middle-class status through insufficient pay and unreasonable working conditions, or a sign of greed, the protection of incompetence, and an unwillingness to work hard. Teachers' unions are a matter of considerable controversy in America, but if you live in a state and a district where membership is offered to you, there are two very important points to keep in mind.

First, if you are a new teacher, your highest priority is to keep your job. If you have the ability to join a union in your district, you should do it because the union will offer you protections against being terminated that you wouldn't have without the collective bargaining strength of the union. If tenure is offered in your state, your goal will be to work toward that designation, which in most states takes three to five years. If you are granted tenure, it does not mean you have the guarantee of a job for life, but it requires the district to follow a system of due process in order to terminate a tenured teacher.

Remember that teachers are also bound by the responsibilities specified in the contract, and the existence of collective bargaining at your school does not signify the assumption that your administrators have a malicious intent. They have a job to do, and it is reasonable for them to operate under the idea that earning their job as an administrator entitles them to attempt ideas, techniques, and philosophies that they believe are in the best interest of students. Since the interaction between teachers and students is the cornerstone of the educational process, the new ideas brought forth by administrators often require a great deal of action on the part of teachers.

Quite often these actions fall under the category of professional responsibility, but other times the implementation of an administrative plan calls for an unreasonable disruption of the normal responsibilities of a teacher. In these cases, the contract provided by the collective bargaining of the teachers' union creates a necessary balance between all that administrators would like teachers to do, and what is reasonable for teachers to do in order to best serve the needs of their students. Union rules protect teachers, and you need as much protection as possible as a new teacher.

You should enroll in the union if it's offered in your district in order to help maintain a reasonable balance between administration and teachers.

The second main point is that you need to be aware that union activity can be highly offensive to some members of the public, especially if your district is experiencing economic hardship. In addition, some (not all) administrators take union activity personally, especially if a certain administrative plan is opposed by the union. Showing any form of dissatisfaction in public, such as picketing or negative statements to the media, can erode your relationship with your administrators and the community at a point when your career depends on their support and goodwill.

As a new teacher, you should enroll in the union but avoid public displays of protest that might give administrators, parents, and community members a negative view of your professionalism. The appropriate time to become involved in union events in a more active capacity is after you have earned tenure and have built a record of accomplishments and professional conduct. Until then, join the union but stay out of the spotlight to protect yourself and your career.

LESSON:

Physical Setting of Your Classroom

If you are fortunate enough to be assigned a classroom of your own, you may walk into it for the first time before the start of the school year and find all the supplies in boxes and the furniture in a pile in the center of the room. Do not let this frustrate you; instead, view it as an opportunity to arrange the room in a way that reflects your own teaching style and maximizes the engagement of your students. You have the chance to make the physical surroundings of your students welcoming and positive, and it will set the tone for the way students will behave toward you as well as toward their fellow students.

The atmosphere you create, including your physical surroundings and your demeanor, will be reflected back to you by your students.

Arrange the room in a way where all students can see each other, the screen, the board, and you at all times to maximize engagement. Above all, ask yourself if your classroom environment is one in which you would want to spend your time if you were a student. It should be welcoming, neat, and orderly, but also stimulating, with interesting visual items to indicate that your room is a place of learning. As the owner of the room, you have the power to set the tone for how students will perceive the experience of spending time in it.

When students walk into any room, they are immediately faced with signals all around that give an indication of how the room's owner regards them. If the room shows that an effort was made to make the atmosphere interesting and comfortable, it is a compliment to the people who enter it. It's an indication that the owner of the room is happy that the guests are there. A messy, disorganized room—or one that is barren and appears to lack any preparation or forethought—reflects indifference toward the guests on the part of the owner.

The tone of the classroom is the responsibility of the teacher, not the students.

LESSON:

When You Need Help with Supplies and Equipment

Create and maintain a positive relationship with your school's secretarial, technical, and custodial staff members. They will play a large role in your life.

Show some genuine respect for their particular skills and the roles they play in your school. You will get better results by asking for their expertise rather than impatiently making demands. Keep in mind that everyone wants to take pride in his or her job, so honest appreciation for your colleagues on the support staff goes a long way.

Never assume that you outrank anyone, and never behave as if you think you do.

Chapter 4

How to Plan Your Lessons
and Keep Records

Make sure that all material being assessed has been covered thoroughly by the teacher.

—twelfth grader

I like it when teachers care about what they're teaching and put effort into their lesson plans.

—eleventh grader

Stay organized—don't lose students' work!

—twelfth grader

Don't pretend to read their work—ALWAYS do it! If you're not willing to read it, don't assign it.

—twelfth grader

Know your standards!

—principal, grades six to twelve

Don't be discouraged if your plan doesn't go exactly as you had expected—some of my most successful lessons happened that way.

—untenured teacher

LESSON:
Curriculum

Your state will have a curriculum guide available online, and your district may have an even more specific set of standards and topics for each course. Never do your students the disservice of failing to address concepts and skills that they were supposed to learn in your course.

Before the start of the school year, map out the time frame for each topic throughout the year so that you are sure you will be able to cover the entire curriculum with your students.

LESSON:
Character Education

Teachers spend a lot of time with their students; in certain cases they spend more time with students than some of their parents do. This gives teachers a certain opportunity—even responsibility—to help their students avoid potential difficulties that can take place throughout their lives. Character lessons shouldn't be religious in a denominational sense, especially in a public school, but instead should stress themes that can be universally agreed upon as positive. For example, the teacher can tell a story, lead a discussion, or assign a group project about why it's important to see the world from another person's perspective, or about how our actions can affect others. This can be effective in the effort to minimize bullying as well.

It is important to remember, though, that your curriculum standards should always come first, and you should use character education sparingly and as a supplement to your courses' academic material. You can also implement character lessons in ways that maximize student engagement, such as having students lead discussions or complete group projects concerning the ways that each character lesson impacts their lives.

As always, the teacher's own conduct is the most effective character lesson of all. When you react to adversity with integrity and honor, students notice and are influenced positively by it.

LESSON:
Lesson Plans

You should have a lesson plan with, at minimum, objectives, procedures, and the state standards covered for every class, every day.

The core of your lesson plan should be an objective that indicates student action; for example, "Following this lesson, students will be able to . . ." Early in your career, you'll need to complete a full lesson plan that adds to the objectives with procedures, materials, time estimates, essential questions, and standards.

Some districts prefer their teachers to put lesson plans in the form of learning targets. In this style, the objective is written from the point of view of the student, beginning with the words "I can." For example, "I can analyze the impact of the Neolithic Revolution on the development of civilization."

The learning targets for each day should be clearly posted in your classroom so that students are always aware of what they should be learning during that class. In order to be sure the objective has been met, some teachers like to use the strategy of an "exit ticket" for each student, in which the students write the answer to an essential question concerning the objective and hand it to the teacher on the way out of the classroom.

LESSON:
Substitute Plans

Leave a set of all-purpose plans for a substitute in a location where they can be easily located. They should consist of a period-by-period description of each course, grade level, and seating arrangement, along with class rosters and an assignment that is relevant work for the students regardless of the time of year. This is beneficial in the event that you have an emergency that requires you to be out of school without warning.

An effective way to do this is to leave a review assignment that deals with material from the start of the school year so that students can benefit from reviewing it. Make it an assignment that can be completed independently and quietly at their seats, and leave a note that you will check the completion and quality of the students' work when you return.

If you have advance warning of your absence, you can leave an assignment that is more timely than your all-purpose one, and then hide the emergency teaching plans until you return. In addition, your individual school will likely have a substitute guide for you to fill out, and you should be sure to fulfill the requirements for your district. Some districts require teachers to find their own substitutes, and others utilize office staff for that purpose, but it is always a good idea to plan as far ahead as possible.

LESSON:
Setting Up Your Gradebook

Most districts have software with your gradebook online so that a portion of it can be viewed by parents. Check with your department chair, technology director, or one of your colleagues in order to obtain access to your online gradebook. At minimum, it will include a list of students in each section along with absences and calculations of their average in your class for the marking period and the year. In order to accomplish this, there will be a method for you to input assignments, a specific weighting formula to calculate averages, and a section for teacher comments.

Here are two important points to remember about setting up your gradebook: (1) access it as soon as possible to familiarize yourself with how it works and (2) purchase an old-fashioned paper gradebook in which you will write the class rosters, along with their assignments, tests, and grades. This allows you to walk around your room with it and input grades while you check students' work, and you can bring it to meetings about a particular student's progress.

Even though those actions can also be accomplished with a portable electronic device, the paper copy also serves as an important backup in the event that something goes wrong with the online gradebook and the assignments and grades are lost. Make no mistake—this has happened to more than one teacher, and it can cause a lot of trouble. You should transfer the information from your paper gradebook to the online version as quickly and as often as possible so that your grades remain up-to-date.

LESSON:
Communication

Use your district's online technology to keep parents and students informed about their progress throughout the year.

The fewer surprises that students have at the end of the marking period, the better, because they will have more time to address any trouble with their performance in your class. Teachers can help students avoid failing by noticing potential problems early and correcting them before the students' final grades are jeopardized.

If you use written communication with your students or their parents, be especially careful of your spelling and grammar. This idea also applies to anything you ever write, including memos, e-mail, notes on the board, PowerPoint presentations, permission slips, handouts, assignments, tests, and any written communication whatsoever. An error in spelling, grammar, punctuation, or usage—even if it is the result of a typo—can seriously damage the credibility of the teacher. Take the time to check everything you write very carefully.

LESSON:

Turnaround Time and Diligence

Take the time to read student assignments, score their tests, and post their grades with as little turnaround time as possible.

We live in a time when people have come to expect that many aspects of their lives will be available for them to access "on demand." When students turn in an assignment, project, or test, all other aspects of modern life lead them to expect that they will discover their results very quickly. If that does not happen, the diligence of the teacher is called into question in the minds of students and their parents. In turn, the motivation of students to complete their work is now diminished.

That does not mean you should rush through the scoring process without thoroughly evaluating the students' work. On the contrary—if students get the impression you are not reading their assignments and tests thoroughly enough, the quality of their work will decrease. In fact, you will most likely encounter students who feel that they have the ability to turn in work with irrelevant information or "joke" answers. Some of them are eager to brag about this to their classmates, and it results in significant damage to the teacher's integrity and credibility. At all costs, do not ever let this happen.

Chapter 5

How to Start the School Year

Teach in a way that you would want to be taught.

—eleventh grader

The influence teachers have over students also means they have the power to tear them down.

—twelfth grader

I like it when teachers are funny.

—eighth grader

Talk WITH students, not AT them.

—ninth grader

Always be kind to your students, even when you feel down yourself.

—twelfth grader

Always lock your door when you're not in the room.

—twelfth grader

LESSON:

Greet Your Students

Own the room! A good way to establish that the room will follow your positive, optimistic example is to greet your students at the door.

Make each student feel as if he or she plays an important role in the atmosphere you have created. You can set the tone immediately by greeting each student at the door. If you position yourself in the doorway, you can monitor everything that is taking place in your classroom as well as in the hallway. This is important, because teachers are responsible for the safety of their students, and the presence of teachers in the hall reduces the chances for trouble. A practical tip: keep your room key with you at all times when you're in school. It will save a lot of embarrassment if, for any reason, your classroom door becomes locked with you on the outside. It is especially humiliating if your students are in the room at the time, so be proactive and keep your key with you.

LESSON:
Cultivate Respect

Show the students that you like spending your time with them in your classroom. Don't ever give them an indication you'd rather be somewhere else.

Avoid statements about hating Mondays and looking forward to weekends. It gives students the idea that spending time in your classroom is a negative experience. If you consistently indicate to your students that you look forward to your time together, it cultivates a positive impression of your class and your course. It may take some time, but you have to make your students believe you. To do that you must believe it yourself.

Your positive approach cannot be cynical manipulation. While you cannot always be in a good mood, look back to the earlier section of this guide for the advantages of the teaching profession, especially the importance of the role you play in the lives of your students. Do whatever you have to do to stay positive, and make sure it is genuine.

One way to show your students that you appreciate their presence in your classroom is to dress and behave in a professional manner. Your clothing and grooming do not have to be overly formal, but your appearance should reflect the importance you're placing on your position as their teacher, and a professional appearance is a sign of respect for the people around you.

Similarly, your behavior in front of your students does not need to be overly formal; your goal is to build connections with your students that will increase their motivation to perform well in your class. However, it is possible to establish a bond with them without behaving in a childish, obscene, foolish, or overly familiar manner. Your students will respect you more if your balance of kindness, humor, and seriousness of purpose gives your students a standard of behavior they will look up to and want to emulate.

Within those parameters, you should make every effort to allow your individuality to dominate both your demeanor and your policies. Just as some students respond better to certain teaching methods compared to others, some students also respond better to certain personalities.

Within reason, teachers need to display their own unique practices and expectations in order to serve the needs of all students.

Both in higher education and the world of work, students will eventually encounter instructors and bosses with dramatically different expectations and personalities. One of the best gifts we can give students is the experience of dealing with a wide spectrum of personalities and classroom procedures among their teachers.

LESSON:
Punctuality and Behavior

As teachers, we expect our students to be on time, stay on task, and show respect for others. If we expect that from the students, we should display those same qualities in full view of our students. Make sure you are one of the first teachers to arrive in the morning, and one of the last to leave. Punctuality and the time you devote to your work always reflect well on you as a professional, and administrators look on it very favorably.

It also shows students, colleagues, and administrators that your career is important to you. Arriving early gives you the opportunity to arrange your classroom for the day's lessons without feeling rushed, and staying late allows you to complete a great deal of work and tie up loose ends.

As far as the other rules of the building, it has a tremendous impact when teachers follow the rules of conduct meant for students and avoid flaunting the fact that they are not required to do so. For example, if there is a school rule against students eating or drinking in a classroom, don't eat or drink in front of students. If it is against the rules for students to be late to your class, make sure you are on time for your classes as well. If it is against the rules for students to cut to the front of the cafeteria line, you yourself should wait in line along with the students, even though you can get away with cutting to the front. It is true that the time a teacher has to eat is usually very short, but the character that you're demonstrating to your students overrides the inconvenience to you.

Your students will be significantly more motivated to follow the rules of your school as well as the ones you create for your classroom if you are conspicuously following them yourself.

LESSON:

Availability

In addition to providing a positive example by arriving early, staying late, and demonstrating respect for the rules, very few actions on the teacher's part will send as powerful a message as making yourself available for helping your students. Quite frequently, students will need clarification on your course material. Students often have a busy schedule, and as a new teacher, you most likely have limited extra time as well. However, if a student approaches you for help, make whatever sacrifice you have to make, within reason, in order to accommodate that student.

Sometimes it is not possible for you to do so, but if you are able to set aside your personal tasks to help a struggling student, your credibility and reputation as a caring, selfless professional will grow among the school and community for sacrificing your time in this manner. It also contributes significantly to your connection with your students, which greatly improves their cooperation, motivation, and loyalty.

Conversely, if you refuse to help a student, even if the request for your personal time seems unreasonable, it can send a powerful and inaccurate message to your student that you do not care about his or her progress. In addition, word will spread that you are not willing to help students, and your reputation will be damaged. This is one of the fastest ways to cause a negative perception of your professionalism among the students and the community.

IN PRACTICE: You are a new teacher, sitting in your room with your curriculum materials spread out in front of you, trying desperately to complete formal lesson plans in time for an upcoming observation by an administrator. You hear a knock at the door and open it. It is one of your students, claiming to be having trouble with an assignment and asking for your help. What is your response?

1. "I'm really busy right now—I can't help you."
2. "I'm really busy right now—let's arrange a time when we're both free so that I can help you later."
3. "Show me what you're having trouble with—I'll help you all that I can."

The first option is certainly the truth, since you are legitimately occupied with a task that will have a significant impact on your career, and you really cannot spare the time. The problem is that the student does not know this and will feel rejected and pushed aside if you respond in this manner. You may feel as if you are under a great deal of stress, but the student may very well feel the same way and is looking to you as a means to gain understanding and alleviate the stress.

The second option seems reasonable, because you are showing a willingness to help the student at some point. However, you will be giving up the opportunity to gain a great deal of credibility and goodwill on the part of the student, which will spread quickly to other students. Delaying your assistance may still seem to the student to be a brush-off.

The third option is sometimes a painful choice to make, because it involves a major inconvenience on your part. However, the value of helping a student cannot be overemphasized, both for your connection with the student and to the perception of your professionalism in the community. More than one teacher was in a similar situation, and chose the first option. Unfortunately, word often reached administrators with the misleading idea that the teachers were rude and unwilling to help students, which significantly damaged their reputation with the administration.

Making yourself available to help students will significantly contribute to your reputation for professionalism. Put aside personal tasks, within reason, to place student assistance as a priority.

LESSON:

Classroom Rules

Always review and explain the rationale for the rules of your classroom with your students.

Classroom rules should be as few and as brief as possible. Never make a rule you are not willing to enforce. All the rules should center around the theme of treating each other and the teacher with respect, and you should be sure to post them so that students can be reminded of them at all times.

LESSON:

Your Approach to the Rules

Your approach to the rules of the school and classroom should be that you are hoping for the students to comply, but you will definitely enforce the rules if students break them. The term "expectation" is used incorrectly by some teachers, who believe it is a synonym for "demand." Instead, the word should indicate that you genuinely expect that the students are going to follow the rules. Very few things are as frustrating to a student as when a teacher seems to assume the worst intentions on the part of the student.

Being suspicious does help you guard against being taken advantage of, but those suspicions should never be apparent to the students. On the other hand, if you demonstrate that you believe the best intentions on the part of your students, they can sense it and will be much more likely to comply with the rules so as not to betray your trust.

On the first day, it is a good idea to tell the students something that you are going to do, such as passing out a form at a certain time or performing any other small act, then proceed to do exactly what you said you were going to do. This shows the students that when you say something, it has value, and you are willing to back up your words with action. It works best when it is something positive, like promising the students that when they finish their classwork that you will do a class activity that they like.

When you follow through, you establish credibility, without having to resort to punishments or other negative actions. Your students are more likely to follow the classroom rules because they expect that you will stand behind those rules.

As you are deciding on classroom rules, be sure to allow students to maintain basic needs without excessive suspicion on your part. Unless it violates your school's rules, allow students to use the restroom, visit the nurse, and gain access to water. If any individual student abuses this privilege, you can speak to the student about it and consider placing restrictions on that particular student. This discussion should always be private—never confront a student on such a potentially embarrassing matter in front of other students.

Proceed carefully, because personal and medical issues can play a role in a student's requests for the restroom, nurse, or water fountain, and challenging a student on this issue when the student has legitimate cause for the request can result in permanent harm to your credibility with the student.

Just as damaging is the fact that the student, if wrongly accused on this sensitive issue, will be deeply offended and humiliated in a way that causes resentment that the student will remember forever.

IN PRACTICE: You are a new teacher chaperoning a group of twelfth-grade students on a field trip with a colleague who has been teaching for over thirty years. During the long bus ride home, two female students approach you and ask to stop the bus at the nearest service station so that they can visit a restroom. The veteran teacher overhears and angrily rejects their request, accusing them of the ulterior motive of wanting to smoke a cigarette. They turn again to you and implore you to grant their request, telling you that it is an emergency. What do you do?

1. Tell them that you'll ignore your more experienced colleague and stop the bus.
2. Tell them that you'll defer to your experienced colleague's judgment and refuse to stop the bus.
3. Tell them that you'll confer privately with your colleague and let them know your decision.

It is tempting to choose the first option, because the students are convincing and no one wants to be wrong when questioning the validity of someone's need to use a restroom. The problem is that by complying with the students' request, you would undermine the authority of your colleague and run the risk of the students using the opportunity to smoke. If you choose the second option, and the students actually have a restroom emergency, your decision may cause humiliation that lasts a lifetime.

The young teacher chose the third option and asked to speak privately with the veteran teacher. He told his experienced colleague that he was uncomfortable denying the students' ability to use the restroom because the possible consequences of the denial could be worse than the possible consequences of trusting the students. The veteran teacher was still skeptical, but stopped the bus as a favor to the young teacher. With this approach, the new instructor went forward with the least potentially damaging decision, while still displaying respect and deference for his experienced colleague.

Establish and follow the rules, but keep the process as positive as possible.

IN PRACTICE: You were a high-achieving student who, after graduating from your public school system, earned a college degree and certification to become a teacher. A long-term substitute position opens in your area of certification in your former high school, and your district is happy to hire you for a semester. Your principal tells you that since you are young, you will have to establish your authority immediately, laying down the law on the first day so that everyone will know who is in charge.

It is your first day and your schedule consists entirely of twelfth graders. How do you establish the classroom rules?

1. "You seem like good people—I don't think we need to talk about rules."
2. "You seem like good people—here are a few simple rules and how they will help us have an enjoyable and productive semester."
3. "Ok, listen up! It's no secret that you don't like me, and I don't like you, but here's how it's gonna be . . ."

It is good to give the students a vision of themselves that is positive, and they will usually try to live up to that image. However, if you avoid any discussion about expectations, it gives students the impression of excessive leniency. The second choice is the most effective approach, because it combines optimism with the expectation of a productive environment in the classroom. Does the third choice seem too extreme to be real? Unfortunately, this is an exact quote, according to the students.

The new teacher in this scenario was a well-meaning, hardworking person who took the advice of her boss a little too literally. The students walked into their next class and immediately said to the veteran teacher, "You need to do something about the new teacher. We were going to give her the benefit of the doubt and cooperate with her, but she came in practically declaring war. What are we supposed to do? Now we can't help ourselves—we have to go against her!"

The experienced teacher implored them to cooperate and give her a chance and to put themselves in the place of a new teacher trying to find the right tone, not to mention the expectation of a certain level of respect and cooperation granted to any teacher. Unfortunately, both the degree of insult and idea of self-restraint were too much for them, and they drove the teacher out within days.

The idea of a self-fulfilling prophecy really exists. Give the students a vision of themselves that they want to live up to.

LESSON:

Structure

Choose a more orderly seating arrangement and more structured lessons at the start of the school year in order to establish that your classroom is a place where work is accomplished. As the year progresses, you can move to more nontraditional methods with less risk of disruption. A square arrangement of student desks makes class discussions better, since everyone can see each other.

In addition, seating students in alphabetical order around the square helps eliminate many potential problems with excessive socializing. Some might consider the arrangement too impersonal, but the regimentation is more than counteracted by the teacher's ability to remember the students' names more quickly because of the alphabetical seating, as well as the logistical benefits of distributing and collecting work that is already alphabetized.

LESSON:

Student Safety and Drills

Parents and guardians should be able to have a reasonable expectation that when they put their child on the bus in the morning to go to school he or she will be protected from harm to the best ability of school officials until the child gets off the bus after school in the afternoon. In return for this responsibility, school officials have slightly more latitude to infringe on a student's privacy than a law enforcement official.

As an example, in order to search student lockers without their permission, a school principal only needs to meet the standard of "reasonable suspicion," whereas a law enforcement officer would need to meet the more stringent standard of "probable cause," which according to the Fourth Amendment needs to be accompanied by a written warrant from a judge. Teachers and other school officials need to take this responsibility seriously and do everything in their power to keep students safe, with each student's whereabouts accounted for when under their supervision.

School shootings and other dangerous and even deadly situations have gained a great deal of attention in the past decade. School districts have responded by putting into place various emergency procedures in order to minimize the potential for harm. It's very important for you to familiarize yourself with your school's procedures for student safety and follow them to the letter.

Various events may cause blood or other bodily fluid to be present in your classroom. Under no circumstances should students be allowed to be near these fluids. Isolate the spill (or the student) and follow your school's procedures for medical help for the student and for a member of the custodial staff to clean up the fluid. Do not go near the spill or allow students near it until the area can be cleaned and sanitized by appropriate staff members. Familiarize yourself with your school's official procedures regarding potentially hazardous materials before the first day of school. If you are not sure if the fluid is dangerous, you should always take the safe approach by treating every spill as hazardous.

Before the first day that students enter your room, make sure you have reviewed your school's procedure for various drills, such as fire, hurricane, lockdown, lockout, and hold-in-place. Different districts have various names for these drills, and it is imperative that you learn what each alarm signal sounds like, along with the correct procedure. Describe those procedures to each class on the first day. When the alarm signals happen, direct the students as calmly and confidently as possible. Remember, your job in any emergency situation is to de-escalate tension, avoid confusion, and do whatever is necessary for the safety of your students.

Teachers are often among the most trusted individuals in a student's life. A student may confide information to a teacher that gives the impression the student may be in danger of being harmed, by him- or herself or possibly others. As a teacher, you have a legal responsibility to take action to help the student.

Even if you promised confidentiality to the student, you need to notify your school psychologist, sociologist, or guidance counselor immediately. Your student's conversation with you might be a cry for help, and you have an important responsibility to obtain assistance for the student that overrides any promises you made about keeping secrets. Make no mistake, the validity of your word is important in all other aspects of your role as a teacher, but the life of your student is more important.

LESSON:

Stop Bullying Before It Starts

The problems associated with bullying have continued to receive national publicity, and with good reason.

IN PRACTICE: An eighth-grade teacher had a student early in his career whose unusual appearance and slight stature made him a natural target for bullies. Teachers would intervene when they could, but the victim often seemed to bring negative attention to himself through outrageous statements, which later resulted in physical assaults when teachers were out of view.

This occurred decades ago, when the consequences of bullying were not taken as seriously as they are now as the result of increased awareness. In fact, much of the school's attention seemed to be on the outlandish behavior of the victim. A deal was made to let him build model cars and airplanes under the teacher's supervision, so the teacher spent considerable one-on-one time with the student and gained some insight concerning the victim's point of view. He asked the teacher to explain why people treated him so badly and wondered if any of the things he said in an attempt to make people laugh should really cause him to get physically assaulted.

In that moment, the teacher understood that the student, like all of us, was searching for a way to get acceptance, appreciation, and respect. It would be satisfying to report that the student was able to overcome his problems, but that is not the case. The bullied student was desperate for friends and to be accepted and appreciated by anyone.

One summer night, he followed several of the students who had mistreated him to a lake, where one of them jumped in the water with his clothes on and began struggling. The bullied student jumped in to save him, but he himself was taken by the undertow and swept out into the lake. It was days before his body was found. The lines at the funeral home were so long that they stretched around the block. The bullied student finally received his acceptance, appreciation, and respect. Unfortunately, it was far too little, far too late.

Bullying is a problem that deserves the attention it has been getting, and teachers need to do everything in their power to stop it. There are a lot of things that happen between students when adults are not watching.

More recently, awareness has been raised about the effects of bullying. In one district, the school psychologist distributed a survey so that students could provide information about the nature and extent of their bullying problem. What do you think the survey revealed?

1. There isn't a serious problem with bullying.
2. Many of the students are being bullied, mainly by other students.
3. Many of the students feel that they are being bullied by teachers as well as students.

It may surprise you, but the third option is correct. While the teachers believed they were setting a high standard—and it is important to do so in an academic sense—the students perceived that their personal relationships with some of their teachers are characterized by inflexibility, lack of empathy, and cruelty. Those attributes have nothing to do with rigorous academic standards. Undoubtedly, the teachers would be shocked to hear this, and many faculty members in that particular district certainly were, but it underscores the idea that students sometimes receive a message the teacher never intends to send.

Be cognizant of the impression you are making on your students. They look up to you, and your words and actions are powerful.

IN PRACTICE: So, as a teacher, you are now in possession of this information and awareness about the toxic and often tragic effects of bullying. How do you address your students in order to stop bullying most effectively?

1. Tell students that bullying is wrong, then immediately back up that statement by making every student who bullies someone face the consequences according to school policies.
2. Tell stories about students who have been mistreated with tragic consequences, so that everyone is aware of the magnitude of what is at stake.
3. Treat every one of your students with dignity and respect, modeling the way students should treat each other, knowing that the tone you create in your room will be reflected back in the form of students' behavior.

In this case, all three options should be put into practice by every teacher.

Chapter 6

How to Present Your Material Effectively

Don't be boring!

—ninth grader

Explain the material thoroughly, because sometimes students don't understand even if they won't admit it.

—twelfth grader

Competition makes learning more interesting.

—twelfth grader

Don't get too off-topic.

—seventh grader

Take the time to answer the question, "Why are we learning this material?"

—faculty colleague

Bring food.

—ninth grader

Make sure you're standing when you present material to students.

—twelfth grader

Good teachers know their material, but great teachers know how to teach their material.

—eleventh grader

LESSON:

Inspiration

There is a reason why you chose to be a teacher of the subject you are teaching—it is because you love the material. Make sure your students see why you love it.

There is a saying among salespeople: "ABC," as in "Always be closing," indicating that the salesperson should be constantly moving the customer toward completing the deal. In the profession of teaching, the expression should be "ABS," or "Always be selling," because the teacher should never stop explaining the importance of the material being studied by the class. Think of the real-world applications for the subject and give the impression that you are accomplishing something important together for the betterment of the students' lives, our nation, and the world in general.

Are you having trouble finding something important enough to sell the topic to your students? If that is the case, you should ask yourself why you are teaching it. At the very least, the topics you are covering are in your curriculum, and they are included there for a reason. Are those topics building the necessary information and skill to help students become informed, engaged, and capable adults? The answer is surely yes, or those topics would not be in the curriculum.

At minimum, the material and skills you are covering are required for your course and are most likely measured on a state test. At maximum the students will take the lessons into adulthood and make a better world. This principle also applies to classroom activities, assignments, homework, projects, and anything else you ask students to do. Whatever it is, always explain the importance of the task and the benefit students will gain from completing it, and repeat this explanation often.

There is a debate in the field of educational psychology about whether intrinsic or extrinsic approaches are more effective to achieve motivation on the part of students. The answer is that they both should be used in order to achieve the most student engagement. Extrinsic motivation already exists in schools in the form of grades, and various kinds of incentives can be useful for teachers to motivate students and to lead them to the necessary course material.

Ultimately, however, the goal should be to bring about the kind of intrinsic motivation in which students develop a curiosity about your subject and want to know more about it. This is why it is crucial for teachers to convey to their students their own deep fascination with their subjects in order to inspire their students to view the material in the same way. Students know that their teachers had to go to college to learn about their subjects and that they have life experience. When the teacher shows a strong interest in his or her course material, students gain the impression that there must be validity to it and often the result is the teacher passing his or her enthusiasm and fascination with the subject on to the students.

LESSON:

Keep Their Minds Working

All students, from the highest achieving to the least motivated, crave intellectual stimulation. If they do not get it from you and your lesson, they will be tempted to get it by disrupting and undermining you and your lesson.

Competitive games help keep students interested and involved. Refer to appendix A for a description of review activities that keep students engaged.

LESSON:

Make It Relatable

One of the reasons why it's important for teachers to make connections with their students is so that the teachers gain insight into the interests of their students. This in turn allows them to present the course material in a manner that is interesting and engaging to their students. Teachers who neglect to do this are forfeiting the opportunity to reach their students, who might otherwise lose interest.

One technique is to use an analogy, where you compare the point you are trying to make with an action the students are familiar with in their own lives. For example, the subject of economics contains the fundamental concept of opportunity cost, which is defined as the specific benefit lost to a business when it chooses one action over another, and the opportunity cost can be quantified with a number. This is an important part of the decision-making process used by businesses, and it's a key concept in economics, so it's crucial that students gain a grasp of the topic in order to have a basic knowledge of the subject.

With that in mind, if you were an economics teacher, how would you describe the concept to your students so that it relates to their lives? You might use the example of students waking up in the morning and deciding what to wear for school. Their clothing options can usually be divided into two categories: casual and formal. If the student chooses casual clothes, like jeans and a T-shirt, he or she may be comfortable but will lose the opportunity to feel sharp, which they would have experienced with formal clothes.

Under this scenario, the opportunity cost of choosing the comfort of casual clothes is the sharp, well-dressed feeling they would have had with formal clothes. Conversely, the opportunity cost of choosing the sharp appearance of the formal clothes is the comfort they would have had if they had chosen casual clothes. It is true that a multinational corporation using the concept of opportunity cost to decide questions of worldwide production is a more complicated question than what is portrayed in the example. However, making a complex issue relatable to the everyday lives of your students can help them gain better initial knowledge and comprehension of the topic, allowing you to move on to the higher-level approaches of analysis, synthesis, and evaluation regarding the concept.

In the course of explaining complex concepts to students, make the information relatable to their lives.

LESSON:

Talent

When you present your material to your students, as you alternate between discovery, student-centered activities, and teacher-centered techniques, consider making use in some way of the talents you have developed throughout your life. For example, if you have artistic ability, create drawings, paintings, bulletin boards, and other visual representations to bring perspective to your students.

If you have musical ability, create review songs to help prepare your students for tests, or intersperse the quick recall of song titles within the review of your course material to sharpen their access to stored information. The effect of this will be to motivate your students by placing the material in a more interesting format, increase their cooperation by making your class more enjoyable, and strengthen the bond between you and your students. It is very important, though, that you use this technique in moderation and with great self-discipline, or risk the loss of credibility and other negative effects that occur when you allow too much time off-task.

Do not be afraid to use your own talents and interests to increase the interest and understanding of your students.

LESSON:

Time on Task

Students often appear eager to lead the teacher to "go off on a tangent," meaning that the teacher will begin discussing ideas, events, or information of any kind that has little or nothing to do with the lesson objectives.

A teacher can utilize these off-topic moments to actually increase student achievement by strategically allowing these tangents to occur, but to contain them to nothing more than a few seconds each. It should be noted that the teacher should avoid interrupting students who are working independently and are on task.

If the off-topic moments are kept to a reasonable length, they can provide a refreshing and humorous temporary break for the students, which helps motivate them to learn and to view your class in a positive light. If the distraction lasts longer than a few moments, or if you allow them to occur too frequently, the lesson can be compromised, along with the dignity, credibility, and reputation of the teacher.

IN PRACTICE: A student walks into your twelfth-grade class with a bag of tiny orange peppers, which the student identifies as habanero peppers. He offers you a small wager: If you can eat an entire habanero pepper without consuming anything else to counteract the uncomfortable effects during the rest of the class period, you win. If you are unable to complete the agreement, the student wins. You are conflicted because you want your class to have seriousness of purpose and rigor, but you also want to find a way to gain the interest, attention, and full participation of your students so that your subject is more appealing to them. What should you do?

1. Confiscate the habanero peppers to eliminate the distraction and immediately begin class.
2. Confiscate the peppers, tell a ten-second anecdote about eating spicy foods, then begin class.
3. You and several students all consume the peppers, causing them all to get sick, resulting in an emergency room visit for at least one of the students.

A case can be made for each of the first two options. Putting a quick end to the distraction allows more time for learning to take place, but this can lead to the impression of humorlessness and inflexibility. If the teacher adds a quick anecdote that is confined to a few moments, the students will have a more positive impression of the classroom, as long as the teacher has enough self-discipline to stop the tangent and return to the lesson objective.

If the interruptions become frequent, the first choice becomes the more appropriate approach. Unfortunately, the teacher in this actual scenario chose the third option, along with the consequences mentioned in the description. It was the wrong choice.

Your time with the students is precious; never give them the impression that you are willing to waste that time with excessive distractions and pointless tangents.

How to Conduct a Discussion

One of the most effective ways to engage students in the learning process is through a discussion. In addition to the course material that you're covering with the discussion, the process allows you to introduce and reinforce several important character lessons as well. One of them is the willingness to respect another person's point of view without necessarily agreeing with it.

Another is the ability to make points about the substance of the debate, rather than resorting to personal insults. Learning how to contribute to a conversation without being overly domineering or refusing to allow others to speak is also important for students to learn, along with a general reinforcement of civility and decency.

One method of discussion involves the teacher posing an "essential question," which is fundamentally important to the main idea of your topic. Ideally, your question should be inquiry based, which is to say that it calls for the higher-level thinking skills of analysis, synthesis, and evaluation.

Students will offer their opinions by taking turns speaking. The teacher should have ground rules in place before engaging in the discussion, after already making the decision as to the level of teacher involvement in the proceeding. Generally, the younger the grade level, the more the discussion should be teacher-led. Enforce rules about civility, appropriateness, and students raising their hands and waiting to be called on before speaking.

Prompt the discussion by asking leading questions that take the conversation in the direction you want in order to maximize the coverage of your curriculum. Be sure, however, that your role in the discussion does not turn into a display of your knowledge for its own sake. Remember that any discussion should be for the purpose of allowing your students to exchange ideas and use the higher-level thinking skills of analysis and evaluation to form their opinions.

Taking and defending a position is an important skill for your students. In the course of doing so, they will have many questions about the issues they are discussing. You may have an extensive academic background in the subject, or you have thorough knowledge of the curriculum because you previously taught the course.

It is all right for you to serve as a source for the knowledge and comprehension bases for the students to build on in a discussion, but avoid doing so only to show the extent of your own knowledge. Keep in mind— it is about them, not you.

For older grade levels, it is beneficial for students to have fewer constraints in their discussion. They should be encouraged to speak freely and to police themselves with regard to civility, appropriateness, the direction of the topics, and deciding whose turn it will be to speak. This seems risky on the part of the teacher, but the most recent versions of teacher evaluations require the observable presence of student-led discussions, and for good reason. As students proceed into adulthood and careers, they are going to need to be able to express themselves in an effective manner while maintaining civility and without waiting to be called upon.

During your discussions, and for that matter at all times, it is imperative that you avoid betraying any bias in your point of view. This is very controversial, and some teachers believe that they serve their students best when they are forthcoming with their own beliefs. The theory is that they are serving to model for their students the act of taking a position and defending it.

This may be true, but any positive effect of it is more than counteracted by the damage it does to a student's own act of developing his or her worldview. If the issue is politics, this is especially relevant. Our job as teachers is to develop the ability of the students to think for themselves and to develop their opinions based on demonstrable facts combined with their own values, experiences, and logic.

Students are aware that teachers have experienced both higher education and years of life experience as an adult, so our opinions carry some weight with them. Do not ever misuse that power, because you will be robbing students of their right to experience the process of evaluation for themselves. It is in the best interest of students to develop their opinions in their own minds without undue influence from you.

The job of a teacher is to teach students how to think, not to think for them.

Lead them to the relevant facts using a wide spectrum of legitimate and verifiable sources, and present both sides of any debate in an evenhanded manner.

Encourage your students to form their own opinions based on facts and their own logic, values, and experiences. Remain objective and avoid bias at all times.

LESSON:

Balance of Thinking and Learning Levels

In order to give students the most useful, effective, and wide-ranging education, teachers must always maintain a balance of higher and lower levels of thinking and learning. The original version of Bloom's Taxonomy ranks activities from knowledge and comprehension (remembering and understanding) as the lower foundation, up through the levels of application and analysis (solving problems and relating component parts), to the higher levels of synthesis and evaluation (creating original ideas and taking and defending a position).

An effective teacher avoids an overemphasis on any one of the levels. For example, requiring students to form opinions without exposing them to facts is not useful for any purpose. Similarly, requiring students to memorize facts without using them for a higher purpose relegates that information to short-term memory, where it is eventually rendered pointless.

When you do require your students to function on the levels of knowledge and comprehension, the most effective way to accomplish this is to challenge the students to find the "critical difference" that separates one definition from another. Then, use that foundation of knowledge and comprehension to challenge your students to think on the high level of evaluation by taking and defending a position based on the information. Doing so will make their learning both meaningful and long-lasting.

Keep all levels of thinking and learning in mind as you plan your lessons, and create a balance where students are using the information in your curriculum for higher-level activities.

LESSON:

Balance of Presentation

Different students learn best in different ways. Some prefer projects in which students work as a team. Others learn best with visual stimulation, and still others are auditory learners. When students work independently of the teacher to obtain the necessary skills and information, whether alone or in groups, it is referred to as discovery-based learning.

When a teacher plays a large role in the transmission of knowledge and skills, in either a lecture or discussion format, it's referred to as a teacher-centered approach. In order to serve your students most effectively, you'll need to plan your lessons to accommodate all styles of learning. Implementing a wide range of strategies for this purpose is called differentiated instruction, and it is important to do everything you can to keep your lessons differentiated in order to reach every one of your students.

Your approach to any topic should be a balance between discovery, student-based approaches, and explanatory, teacher-based discussions to serve the entire spectrum of learning styles.

LESSON:

Group Projects

Group projects can be an effective way for students to become engaged in the learning process and utilize skills that they normally would not use in an academic class to further their learning of your subject.

This type of activity also allows your students to gain important life skills in organizing a team and delegating jobs in order to work together toward a common purpose. When conducting a group activity, keep several important points in mind in order to avoid some of the most common problems with this type of procedure.

Your most important consideration is to be sure that the time and effort you and your students are about to devote to the activity have a proportional benefit in terms of the knowledge and skills gained toward your standards for the course. That way, the time will be justified, because you have a responsibility to be sure your students are gaining all of the knowledge and skills specified by the curriculum of your course throughout the year. If the students gain the sense that their group project is lasting too long without a corresponding gain in knowledge and skills, the credibility of you and your course will be diminished in their estimation.

The next issue is to be sure you arrange the groups with a relatively even mix of ability levels, so that they are all more or less equally capable of successfully completing the project. Also, be sure you don't place students together in a group who have issues between them, because potential conflicts can cause distractions that are detrimental to the students' learning.

Inevitably, some members of each group will be more motivated and capable than others, resulting in some students completing more work than their partners toward the completion of the project. In order to combat this, you can take two measures: first, assign a specific task to be completed by each member of the group. Second, make the grades dependent on their individual effort instead of one grade for the entire group. This prevents a motivated, on-task student from having his or her grade diminished by an unmotivated group member.

LESSON:

Public Speaking

As a part of your balance of presentation between cooperative, discovery-based projects and teacher-centered approaches in order to reach students with various learning styles, you will need to work on the skills necessary to become an effective public speaker.

Lectures, ideally for short periods of time, are an effective way to help your students work on the listening skills they will need for college. They are also the quickest way to directly convey a large amount of the concepts and material in your curriculum to your students.

Your first goal—and most important task—as a public speaker is to gain the goodwill of your audience.

If your students do not want to listen to you, your message will not be received by them, and your time and effort will be wasted. This is a factor that greatly helps you achieve your first goal as a public speaker, on the way to eventually achieving your educational objectives for your students. Tone of voice, enthusiasm, mild self-deprecation, and empathy are all qualities you will want to exhibit immediately as you speak to your students in order to gain their attention, their goodwill, and their assumption of your credibility.

Your first consideration is your voice. If you keep it smooth, friendly, and professional, it makes students want to listen to you. Think of your voice as a musical instrument, and your words as a type of melody. If your pitch stays too consistent, or you constantly repeat a vocal pattern, you will sound like an instrument playing the same note or phrase over and over. This is the quickest way to lose the interest of your students, and possibly put them to sleep. If you use variations in the pitch, tone, volume, and rate of your words in order to emphasize points, you will maintain the interest of your students and by doing so make your presentation much more effective.

Movement on your part is also crucial. Don't speak to your students from a seated position—move around the room and take advantage of the fact that proximity to each individual student helps draw that student in to your presentation. Similarly, eye contact accomplishes this as well. When you look a student directly in the eye, a connection is established with that student that makes him or her much more likely to receive and accept the information you are attempting to convey. Use hand gestures and facial expressions, especially smiling and laughing, to emphasize your points.

Avoid the misuse of language and mispronunciations. No one is perfect, and you should not pretend to be, but if you consistently use words incorrectly or mispronounce them, it gives your students the impression that you are a less-than-credible source of information.

If you make a mistake, admit it without hesitation and move on.

A comment on your part that may seem innocent or humorous to you may be highly offensive to some of your students and will weaken your connection of goodwill and diminish your credibility in their eyes. If you feel the need to lighten an overly serious or unhappy atmosphere with humor, direct the jokes at yourself instead of others. Self-deprecating humor, within reason, is one of the ways to gain the goodwill of your audience.

Do not exhibit special treatment for either males or females, or make comments that would make any student feel as if he or she is not valued as a human being. This includes subtle language that would indicate that you value different demographic or socioeconomic groups over others. This can be difficult to detect in your own behavior, because most of us do not realize that we are displaying various biases, but our unknowing signals can be demoralizing to those who notice.

Take care to avoid bias in your language against classes, races, genders, orientations, or any other group of people.

While speaking to their students, one common but subtle bias often used in language by teachers is to hint that they value academic careers over trade-oriented jobs, which take considerable skill and are necessary for the functioning of our society as well as our everyday lives.

Some of your students are going to become our carpenters, bricklayers, electricians, plumbers, and mechanics. They should never be made to feel as if the validity and importance of their skills are in any way minimized by you or others in the class.

If your public speaking is going to be effective enough to meet your educational objectives, it is important that you show enthusiasm for the topic of your presentation. Enthusiasm is contagious—students know that you have education and experience, and if you are obviously fascinated by the subject you are presenting, it makes your students believe there must be a good reason for your interest. In the process, when you demonstrate enthusiasm for your subject, it motivates your students to want to hear more and to want to gain more information about your curriculum.

The length of your presentation should never be so long that it even strains the attention span of the students who want to pay attention to you. Be sure to pause, check for understanding, ask students for their comments, and engage them in any way possible before continuing with the presentation of information. A brief tangent can even be appropriate in order to refresh the students, as long as you bring the presentation back on-topic after no more than a few moments.

You should be aware that any material you are conveying in this manner is likely to be on the knowledge and comprehension levels of Bloom's Taxonomy and should therefore be used in moderation as a supplement to student-centered assignments, projects, and activities. While you can present material very efficiently in terms of volume of concepts, the amount of it that is retained by students diminishes the longer you speak.

Sharpening your public speaking skills will help your students prepare for future college lectures, increase their listening comprehension, and serve your students who are primarily auditory learners. Then, when you shift the focus from your lecture to a student-led discussion or projects and assignments in which students are analyzing, synthesizing, or evaluating the material, you will have successfully facilitated a well-rounded learning experience for your students. In addition to serving visual, tactile, and auditory learners, you will have led students to think on all levels of Bloom's Taxonomy.

LESSON:

Exceptional Student (Special) Education

Before you begin your first lesson, you need to be aware that your state has laws regarding the rights of special needs students. The programs have a variety of names, including special education or exceptional student education, among others. There are many facets concerning the general idea of extra help and accommodations. Students qualify for the programs through the district's identification process, which usually consists of a combination of referrals by classroom teachers and testing by school psychologists and other professionals.

Students who need extra help in certain subjects, identified through referrals and test scores, engage in the practice called "remediation." This consists of small group instruction by a teacher in specific subjects, and they may or may not include testing accommodations. These sessions are sometimes called "labs," as in Reading Lab or Math Lab. A "504" accommodation occurs when students show, through testing, a physical or cognitive challenge to their ability to handle academic work. They are given testing and instructional accommodations that are enforced by law.

Students with an individual education plan, or IEP, are also given accommodations enforced by law, but those accommodations are extensive enough to warrant a separate diploma, referred to as an IEP Diploma. It is imperative that you familiarize yourself with each student in your classes who has been granted accommodations and that you follow those accommodations to the letter, because failure to do so can result in a significant lawsuit. All of these designations, along with their corresponding laws, vary by state. In addition, the terminology can be different in each area, and it is constantly evolving. It is crucial that you study your district's policies before you begin planning your first class.

You are responsible for the education of all students who have been placed in your classroom, regardless of any potential challenges they bring with them.

LESSON:

English for Speakers of Other Languages

You may also encounter students in your classes who have a limited—or even nonexistent—knowledge of the English language. Different states have different names for these students, such as English for speakers of other languages (ESOL), English language learners (ELL), or English as a second language (ESL). It is your responsibility to serve these students. As a teacher, it is useful if you have a working knowledge of other languages.

If you are not fluent in the original language of your students, there are still several methods you can use to maximize their learning. If your school provides a professional translator, your experience with ELLs will be much easier. However, many districts lack the funding to hire the appropriate staff, and you might be on your own. If so, try to identify a student in the same class who is bilingual, and seat the student or students who have difficulty with English near the bilingual student so that he or she can translate for you.

Make your presentations as visual as possible, so they can comprehend what you are trying to say through a medium other than language alone. You should check frequently with the student or students to make sure they are following the information you are attempting to convey to them. In addition, ask the student, through a student interpreter, about his or her country of origin, then research everything you can about the culture, customs, history, and current events of that country.

Doing so will give you a greater understanding of your student and forge a stronger bond. At the very least, your interest will help the student feel welcome in your class, which, aside from being a humane gesture, has the practical effect of increasing his or her motivation to make a strong effort in your class.

Your instructional strategies should include provisions for the entire spectrum of learners, including those with special needs who are entitled to accommodations, gifted students who are desperate for a challenging

and rigorous approach, students who are learning English for the first time, and everyone in between. As you plan each one of your lessons, do not ever neglect to think deeply about this.

LESSON:

Exchange Students

Students from another country who are visiting your school for a semester or a full year, usually referred to as exchange students, also present a set of challenges for the teacher. The first step toward helping the exchange student have a positive experience in your classroom is to view the situation from his or her perspective. Often, language is a barrier, and you will need to follow the steps listed above in the section about ELL students in your classroom.

In addition to language challenges, the student probably feels alone and unsure of how to proceed through the routine of a school day. Speak to the student, both privately and in front of the class, in a manner that makes the student feel welcome. Offer to help in any way possible, and appoint a student you are sure you can count on to show the exchange student around the school, allow the exchange student to sit at the student's table at lunch, and to help him or her find the appropriate classrooms.

Chapter 7

How to Assess Student Progress

Use a variety of approaches.

—ninth grader

Don't give excessive homework.

—tenth grader

Don't rush students when they need more time on a test.

—seventh grader

No matter what you think, students really do want to use their minds. You just have to give them the opportunity to do it.

—eleventh grader

Don't put material on a test that you haven't covered.

—twelfth grader

Don't expect students to know something if you haven't taught it to them.

—twelfth grader

LESSON:

Use a Variety of Assessments

In a similar manner as your instructional strategies, your assessments should represent a variety of avenues for the students to demonstrate their mastery of the material and skills. Avoid bonus points, extra credit, test curves, and other methods of grade inflation. Instead, concentrate on the essential steps of effective instruction: lead the students to the information and skills for which they will be responsible, help them understand it, then give them an opportunity to demonstrate their mastery of it.

The world of work in which your students will eventually participate demands the ability to carry out assigned tasks within a deadline. When students successfully demonstrate this in your class, they should be given credit for the timely completion of their work. It is important to remember, though, that the students need to know that you will collect their daily written work, read it carefully, and assign grades for the quality and accuracy of their work. If the teacher neglects to do this, the quality of their work will decline.

In addition to written tests and assignments that include grades for both and quality, you can give grades for discussion participation. If some students are withdrawn, take the opportunity to call on those students in a respectful manner in order to draw out their participation. If you call on students who don't volunteer, make sure you avoid doing it in a manner that seems like you are trying to call out their inattention.

Never use public humiliation against a student.

If you give students time in class to work on your assignments, you can be there to answer questions, monitor them to reduce the possibility of cheating, and increase the likelihood of the students completing the work, which will have a positive impact on their completion grades. While it is beneficial for students to have repetition and independent work, try to minimize the amount of homework you assign. Too much work outside of class reduces the time students can spend on extracurricular activities, hobbies, interests, jobs, friends, and family, all of which help students to live healthy, well-rounded lives.

Besides giving students a portion of your class time to complete their assignments, another way to minimize excessive homework outside of class is to avoid assigning "busy work." This is defined as work assigned to students, sometimes in large packets, where skills and information are repeated past the point of benefit to students. The situation is made worse if the teacher neglects to introduce and explain the material at the start of the assignment and review the work with students after they have completed it.

Remember that students deeply resent having their time wasted—in every form. Assignments should be introduced and explained, with their validity and purpose asserted, with every question reviewed at the conclusion, and grades scored for both completion and quality.

If you fail to complete any of these steps, your assignment will, in the minds of your students, be added to their list of time-wasting events, including free time in class, an extreme lack of rigor, and excessive tangents and pointless topics during discussions that are not a part of your curriculum.

Students may not seem to mind at first, and they will often encourage these activities just to see if they can bring them about through their powers of persuasion and manipulation. You should be aware, though, that if this becomes a pattern, students will eventually become contemptuous of you and your class, because they know they are supposed to be gaining the knowledge and skills to unlock the next stages of their lives and their time is at a premium. In their minds, the teacher will lose credibility, which often has a dramatic effect in a negative manner on the level of cooperation on the part of the students.

You will need to set up a weighting system for your grades, such as 40 percent tests, 20 percent quality of daily assignments, 20 percent completion of daily assignments, and 20 percent discussion participation. This is an example—you can set up a weighting system based on what makes sense for your courses, grade level, and procedures.

On the subject of formal tests: ask your students when they have large tests or projects in their other classes and try to plan your test around those other commitments. This also applies to significant events that take place at the school. You cannot please everyone and avoid all conflicts, but the fact that you are making an effort to help students perform better sends a powerful message to them. You want them to be able to concentrate on studying your material, and at the same time you are demonstrating empathy and consideration to the students, and you will eventually find some of that consideration reflected back to you.

In addition, avoid pop quizzes or tests that occur without warning. Test dates should be set long in advance, with as much review as possible preceding the test. Some teachers believe that surprising students with assessments causes the students to stay on top of the material at all times, and this is undoubtedly true in the case of many students. However, the benefit is more than counteracted by the predatory effect of punishing students who are trying to learn but have not grasped the material yet.

Your job is to help students understand the material, not to catch them failing to understand it. If they perceive you as their adversary, many of them will lose their will to put their best effort into your course. Many teachers assume that all students are self-motivated, and no doubt some of them are, but it is important to remember that many other students have stopped caring about their grades as a result of learned helplessness. They believe that nothing they do will be good enough, so they stop trying in order to save their own dignity.

Presenting these students a test without warning does not motivate them to study, rather it provides one more bit of evidence in their minds that the teacher wants them to fail, and they become further demoralized and discouraged. It adds to their perception that they don't belong at their school; that the institution was made for different, more successful people. Many of these students decide that the best way forward is to put their heads down and withstand whatever indignities and abuse the school has to offer until they can drop out, all the while refusing to make even the slightest effort that might give the offending teachers the satisfaction of their compliance.

Similarly, avoid entering a zero in the online gradebook on a test for a student who was absent and can still take the test. Some students are motivated to quickly make up the test in order to avoid ruining their average, but many more students see it as an act of malice on the part of the school and will be even more reluctant to complete any work for that teacher. If a student makes up an assignment for partial credit or makes up a test, be sure to change the student's grade in the online gradebook immediately.

Do not ever allow a mistake on your part to negatively affect a student's grade. For example, if you lost a student's paper, make sure he or she does not experience any lowering of his or her grade as a result. If you make a mistake on the scoring of a test, change the student's grade immediately so that there isn't an adverse effect on the student's average.

If you suspect that the student isn't telling the truth about a potential mistake on your part, give him or her the benefit of the doubt until you have solid evidence that you are right. Otherwise, your accusations against a student who has not done anything wrong almost certainly will damage the trust he or she has in you as a teacher and human being, which in turn will affect that student's level of cooperation in your class.

Once you set a due date for a test or a large assignment, avoid moving that date, especially on the due date itself, except under extreme circumstances. Your word should count for something. If you say that a test will happen on a certain day, students will make sacrifices to prepare for it. If you push back the date on the date itself, you are not demonstrating empathy, but instead showing a disregard for the students who worked hard to prepare for that due date. If you move the date, you have also shown that your word is not something you will stand by and that will damage your credibility.

Tests should be constructed in a manner that requires the student to use a variety of approaches to demonstrate mastery. Objective question types such as multiple choice, matching, true or false, and fill-in-the-blank should be balanced with long answer and essay questions in order to obtain an accurate measure of a student's grasp of the material. Review early and often before tests—students should never be unaware of the material they will be responsible for on any upcoming assessment.

It is far better to help your students understand your course material before you give them the test, rather than reprimanding them if they fail to perform well on the test.

Find a way to reach them, and to make the material understandable so that they can eventually demonstrate their mastery of it successfully.

Never express anger, frustration, or impatience at students for their lack of knowledge or ability—that lack of knowledge and ability is your responsibility to fix, and it is the reason you have a job.

Create several versions of your tests and rotate them to minimize the likelihood of cheating by passing answers to later classes, as well as minimizing the perception on the part of your students that you lack the initiative to revise and update your tests. This is another point on which teachers can have their credibility significantly diminished.

Additional techniques to cut down on cheating include making sure you are present when students are testing, checking before they begin to be sure all review materials are securely out of sight, arranging the seats so that students do not have an easy view of other students' tests, and avoiding a testing style that includes easily copied answers, such as bubbling in a computer sheet or turning in printed pages with the real author's name changed. Make every effort to set up conditions that will make it difficult for students to cheat—it is far better to prevent cheating before it begins than to punish a student after it happens.

If you believe that you have caught a student cheating in any form, be very careful. If you unjustly accuse a student of cheating without sufficient proof, you will permanently damage your ability to have a productive relationship with that student. Claiming a student is dishonest in any situation should only be done as a last resort.

Stop cheating before it begins.

The test grades themselves should be balanced with grades from less stress-inducing class activities like assignment completion, assignment quality, class projects, and discussion participation in order for each student's overall average to represent a genuine reflection of his or her mastery of the skills and concepts in your course.

LESSON:

Scoring

When you create a test, you need to calculate the value of each section. That information should be shared with your students before your test so that they know the relative importance of each section of material and can arrange their studying priorities accordingly. For sections of any assessment that are not objective, and therefore require judgment on your part, you'll need to create a rubric. This is a guide that shows the qualities that need to be present in the essay, project, or performance, along with the potential point values for each of those qualities.

If those aspects of the essay are not met to their full potential, a descending list of point values shows the characteristics associated with each less-than-perfect score. Again, your students need to be in possession of the rubric before they take the assessment so that they are aware of the qualities and characteristics on which they are being scored. Refer carefully to the rubric while scoring, because it will help you avoid bias when completing any subjective assigning of grades.

Late work should always be penalized in some manner, because it is important to reinforce punctuality as a life skill. It is also important to respect the effort and sacrifice for the students who did whatever was necessary to complete the assignment on time. Many of them had extracurricular activities and other commitments they had to prioritize in order to complete your assignment and failing to take that into account is insulting, demoralizing, and a disincentive for their continued diligence.

However, you should avoid giving an immediate loss of all credit. To the unmotivated student, this absolves him or her of all responsibility after the initial due date. It also causes a catastrophic effect on a student's average that can be nearly impossible to overcome, which then reinforces a sense of futility in a student who may already feel disconnected with the school and who is already reluctant to make any effort to complete work.

A better approach is to create a descending scale of credit for the timely submission of work. This can be part of your rubric, and it should be known to all your students from the first day. The best way to accomplish this is to list it on your grading policy that you distribute to all students on the first day. The incremental loss of points gives the students an opportunity to complete the work while still rewarding the students who completed it on time. Complete loss of credit should only be given to an assignment that is still not turned in after the descending point values have been exhausted.

The loss of hope is a powerful force that takes away a student's motivation and often leads to dropping out of school entirely. As a teacher, you'll want to be aware of this phenomenon and do everything in your power to preserve a pathway for every student to achieve success.

Never give up hope for any student, and never let any student lose the prospect of success.

Portfolio Assessment

An effective way to track student progress and assess their growth in your course is to include a portfolio assessment as a portion of your students' overall grade average. You can accomplish this by having the student keep daily assignments in a folder, with you checking them each day for a completion grade.

At the end of a particular period of time, ideally the end of a marking period, collect the portfolios of their work and read through them to give a grade on the quality of their work. The students should always be in possession of a very specific rubric before they begin any of the assignments in the portfolio so that they have a clear idea of the criteria by which they will be scored.

An advantage to this method is that students will receive the credit they deserve in accordance with the effort and care they devoted to the assignments each day. This works best for the types of assignments for which it is difficult to assign a specific numerical grade, such as responses, essays, and defending opinions. Using a portfolio format, the scoring can be done collectively for assignments, using a rubric with criteria. It's important to remember how crucial it is for you to read through the portfolios carefully to be sure your students are making a legitimate effort.

Standardized Tests from Your District and State

During the presidency of George W. Bush, Education Secretary Rod Paige instituted the program called No Child Left Behind, the premise of which is that students should be tested at various grade levels with standardized tests in order to determine areas of weakness to be addressed. Since the number of grade levels during which students were tested increased, so did the number of standardized tests the students were required to take.

During the presidency of Barack Obama, Arne Duncan became the Education Secretary and introduced the program called Race to the Top. This amounted to a doubling-down on the No Child Left Behind philosophy because states were rewarded with money for proving that they implemented a policy of further standardized testing. In addition, the Annual Professional

Performance Review of teachers would depend, in part, on the performance of the individual teacher's students on those standardized tests, measuring both achievement and growth.

Is it a fair system for evaluating teachers when so many factors outside a teacher's influence can affect a student's performance on the tests? It is a moot point, because regardless of the fairness, it is to some extent the reality that every teacher lives with on a daily basis. Your best approach is, rather than complain about it, to do everything in your power to help your students perform to their full potential on the tests.

You should also recognize that beyond your best efforts, the students will have to come through for the sake of their own advancement. Avoid making them so stressed about the tests that they have test anxiety and function below their potential. In addition, you need to be sure you are following the curriculum for your district and the state, because many of the tests reflect those standards. Make sure your students are comfortable with the structure and style of the standardized tests. You can help bring that about by making sure you give them the experience of taking some of their tests in the same format.

This is controversial, because some view this idea as "teaching to the test," which they believe stifles creativity and increases test anxiety. On the contrary—students will have less anxiety when they encounter a test format with which they are familiar, especially because different test styles require different thinking skills and processes.

Instructors who find ways to implement a vast array of creative and engaging learning opportunities for their students are to be commended. However, remember that in large measure the students' futures are dependent on their performance on standardized tests. A balanced approach is the key.

The most effective teachers include relevant thought processes, skills, test formats, and curriculum that help students prepare for standardized tests. They balance these with other worthy educational practices like creative projects, discussions, discovery-based assignments, and evaluative papers in which students take and defend a position.

LESSON:

Some Things Are More Important Than School

There is no doubt that teachers should hold students to a high standard in order to prepare them for college and the world of work and to maintain that high standard consistently. However, there are aspects of life that supersede the importance of consistency, and you will need to develop the wisdom and judgment to know when it is appropriate to make exceptions. For example, if a student needs to attend the funeral of a close family member, give the student extra time without diminishing the grade. It is not appropriate to use the established penalty for late work in that situation. Instead, you will serve as a role model for the student by demonstrating how a decent human being shows empathy and concern.

Some things are more important than school.

As a teacher, you should help students to become healthy, well-balanced people. If your student misses school for a family vacation, instead of scolding the student and giving him or her a hard time, help the student make up the missed work in a reasonable amount of time. If a student is fortunate enough to have a family that goes on vacation, allow him or her to savor the experience. Similarly, avoid scheduling large tests before a vacation that may prevent students from leaving with their families. In addition, avoid assigning a large amount of work for the student to complete during vacation with the idea that they will have time on their hands. This has nothing to do with holding students to a high standard. Students need a break for their psychological well-being, and teachers can benefit because students will be refreshed and better able to take on intellectual challenges when they return.

Try to avoid adding to the misery of your students and lift them up instead.

Chapter 8

How to Keep Order

Punishment makes students less likely to do their work.

—seventh grader

I don't like it when a teacher is mean to me without a good reason.

—eighth grader

Treat your students with respect, and they'll treat you the same way.

—ninth grader

Think of your students as individuals instead of a mass of students.

—ninth grader

Don't punish one student when others are doing the same thing.

—twelfth grader

Respect goes both ways—don't expect your students to respect you if you don't respect them.

—twelfth grader

It's possible to keep discipline and still have fun.

—tenth grader

Motivation

This is the topic that many new teachers feel most apprehensive about as they imagine facing a room full of students for the first time. You do not need to feel stress because of this. It is natural to feel this apprehension, but view the situation in a different way: education is not a war and students are not your enemies. You are not going into battle when you enter your classroom, and the unfortunate teachers who have this mindset spread a great deal of unhappiness, and quite often, the self-fulfilling prophecy happens in which students behave in an adversarial and disrespectful manner toward a teacher who places them in the role of the enemy.

In order to promote an orderly and disciplined classroom, it is important for the teacher to understand what motivates students, as well as humans in general.

We all want acceptance, appreciation, and respect. The best way to achieve that is to forge connections with others based on goodwill.

This gives us a sense of belonging, and we'll use any excuse and take every opportunity to achieve it, positive or negative. The teacher has to provide that connection for students in a positive manner before someone else does, in a way that might not be as positive.

Your Voice

At the beginning of the year, shouting at a student or the entire class to get their attention will most likely startle your students enough to temporarily achieve their compliance, but ultimately this will work against you. If you raise your voice to enforce discipline, it will require increased volume each time you use it as the students develop a tolerance for it. It will not take long before you will have to shout in order to achieve the most basic functions of the class.

Instead, if you keep your voice calm and authoritative over a considerable length of time, students will perceive your words to have more value, and the slightest inflection in your tone will carry more significance for them. At the same time, you will be contributing to the creation of a tone of respect in your classroom, while raising your voice contributes to an atmosphere of chaos and disorder.

A loud voice is also unpleasant to the ear, and the frequent use of it will usually result in an unfavorable impression of your class on the part of your students. This violates the most important rule of public speaking, which is that for your message to be received, you must first gain the goodwill of your audience. Shouting takes you further from this goal, while a calm, reasonable voice brings you closer to it.

Keep your voice calm.

Be careful with the words you choose so that you avoid clichés, mixed metaphors, slander, malapropisms, biased language, and verbal tics. Repeating the same word too frequently and using fillers like "um," "like," and "you know" should be avoided. All of those characteristics result in a significant distraction for students, and they often find it humorous to make a secret tally of the number of times you repeat a word or make a certain mistake.

If you have several words that you use with excessive frequency, students may even secretly play a bingo-style game to see who can identify a winning combination of your too-often repeated words. Another classic is for the students to take bets on the number of times a teacher will repeat a certain word throughout the class period. As enjoyable as these distractions may be for your students, they represent a scenario in which you have lost control of the atmosphere of the room.

It is not always easy for you to recognize when you are committing these mistakes, and many new teachers are surprised when certain verbal and visual bad habits they never suspected they had are pointed out to them. It can be helpful for you to record yourself with audio or video in order to discover these flaws, or to practice making a presentation with a person you trust outside of school to evaluate your speaking style. No matter how you do it, you have to fix these tendencies because they have a tremendously negative impact on your credibility as a teacher.

LESSON:

Be Proactive Instead of Reactive

Instead of waiting for discipline problems to occur and then reacting to them, prevent as many of them as possible before they happen by taking proactive measures. If you do not want students to have too much opportunity to socialize, avoid facing the desks toward each other in small groups and instead arrange them in a square that is conducive to large group discussions.

If you do not want students to write on your board unless it's part of an assignment, avoid leaving the markers on the chalk tray. If you do not want students to access secure materials, keep them locked away far from student reach.

Preventing disorder before it begins is preferable to dealing with problems after they happen, and every problem you avoid makes your classroom a better place.

LESSON:

Authority

However energetic and disruptive some students may appear to be, students generally want security and order. A chaotic classroom is ultimately not enjoyable or productive for anyone, and students are counting on their teachers to create an atmosphere conducive to learning that is comfortable and safe. They want reasonable rules that teachers enforce in an even-handed manner for the benefit of everyone.

At the same time, a teacher who appears to take satisfaction from reprimanding or punishing a student causes a detrimental effect on the motivation and morale not only on the student in question, but the other students who are watching. Most students make more of an effort when there is a positive connection with the teacher asking them to do a particular assignment or comply with simple classroom rules of conduct. This bond occurs most often when the teacher creates an atmosphere of order and security, and at the same time shows empathy, compassion, and concern for the success of each student.

Your demeanor should strike a balance between kindness and authority.

Develop a vision in your mind of how such a teacher would look and sound, then try to live up to that vision. The best teachers find that perfect balance, but it is very difficult to achieve.

IN PRACTICE: You are a twenty-one-year-old student teaching intern, assigned to a class of twelfth graders who have been tracked so that your section is filled with the least-motivated students in the senior class, some of whom are twenty-year-olds who have repeated the grade twice. The bell rings, so you purposefully walk in, try unsuccessfully to slam the door, and in your roughest voice bellow, "All right, everybody sit down!"

At this point your toe hits the corner of a table, and you fall face-first into a row of desks, all of which fall over, with the last one knocking over the movie projector stand. As a final insult, the reel-to-reel film splits in half. The class erupts in laughter while you make your way out from under several desks. How do you address the class?

1. "Excuse me! I could have really been hurt! You should be ashamed of yourselves!"
2. "Everything's under control—nothing to see here!"
3. "Did you see that? I hope someone captured that on video—it was the greatest spill I ever took!"

The first response would make you seem humorless and self-absorbed and would guarantee that students would make fun of you behind your back. The teacher in this scenario actually chose the second option, which is humorous in its own way because it evokes the scene in a Leslie Nielsen movie where he's standing in front of an exploding fireworks factory, telling the crowd, "Nothing to see here!"

The problem is that it is humorous because it is pathetic, which you definitely do not want to be, and only works in your favor if you say it ironically. Unfortunately, the teacher in this scenario did not, and he reports that it must have been fifteen minutes before the laughter died down. The teacher should have picked the third option.

When unforeseen things take place, the laughter is going to happen. It can be behind your back, at you, or with you. It is always better to laugh with your students.

LESSON:

Sincerity

Sincerity wins every encounter.

It beats meanness, sarcasm, hostility, passive-aggressiveness, and even humor. This should be your default attitude toward every situation with students, colleagues, administrators, and parents until extreme circumstances require you to change your approach. If you make a mistake that affects an individual student, admit your mistake and apologize directly to that student. If you make a mistake that affects the entire class, admit your mistake and apologize to the entire class.

The power of this act cannot be overemphasized. The sincerity you show by doing this will have a positive and significant impact on your connection with your students. You are also demonstrating good character to your students, and it will be reflected back to you in the manner in which they choose to handle disagreements with you and with each other.

LESSON:

Planning and Pacing

Make sure you have planned a lesson that will last for the entire class period and move purposefully through that lesson. Keep several short activities ready in the event that you need to fill ten minutes or so at the end of class.

Avoid wasting time before the bell, and do not let students line up at the door before the class period is over.

Every minute you spend with your students is important, so do not give them the impression that any of that time can be discarded.

As previously discussed regarding the subject of lesson plans, make a calendar with the topics you need to cover based on your curriculum mapped out for the entire school year. This helps you avoid spending too much time on some of the course material and not enough on other important topics. For each day's lesson, you should have enough material to cover that you can move through it with a sense of purpose, at a pace that keeps the students intellectually engaged. As you do so, however, be sure to check for understanding throughout the lesson so that you gain a sense of the effectiveness of your pace for the students in the particular class in front of you. It may be different than what is appropriate for other groups of students.

LESSON:

Never Give an Ultimatum

Don't ever give an ultimatum to your students.

It is much more effective to give the class a goal with a concrete reward for reaching it, such as every student completing an assignment. Then, make sure you fulfill your promise. Never call out a student directly—it forces the student to save face by putting on a show of defiance.

Disruptive behavior should be handled calmly through direct conversation with the student, away from the view of the rest of the class.

Under normal conditions, a class will only take pleasure in your discomfort if you act like you are above everyone else. Showing magnanimity at a time when the student needs a break will most often be rewarded by gratitude, respect, and loyalty on the part of the student in the future. You have the ability to crush him; you don't need to prove it. If the behavior occurs again, speak to the student privately to remind him or her of your expectation of respect.

IN PRACTICE: You are a relatively new ninth-grade teacher, and you have taken great care to set up your classroom in an orderly, comfortable arrangement conducive to class discussions. As the class works on an assignment, a male student slides his desk several feet so that it is adjacent to a female student's desk. You would like to keep the room in order, so you approach the male student and ask him in a calm and friendly voice to please move his desk back where it belongs. He responds by staring at you in silence, and does not move. What should you do?

1. Ignore the situation, since the student is not really causing a disruption.
2. In a reasonable and quiet voice, ask him to speak to you after class.
3. Tell him to move his desk back within five seconds, or he is going to have to report to the office.

The first response can work, but only if the student is actually not causing a disruption, in which case, you did not need to ask him to move. You also run the risk of demonstrating to the class that if you make a request from a student, it is not necessary for the student to comply. Sometimes, developing the wisdom to know how to choose your battles, along with the time and place for them, can be the most valuable information to have as a teacher.

The second choice preserves the dignity of the student and keeps the class moving, while still showing the class that your words have credibility without the showdown that comes with an ultimatum. The perception that if you say something it is not necessarily important can be the first step on a slippery slope toward a class treating you with disrespect.

The third option is practically the definition of an ultimatum. The student feels as if the entire class is watching him—and they are—so he cannot allow himself to give in. The student will respond to you in a completely different manner under these conditions, and it is in the interest of both you and the student to have the conversation at a different time, when the student's peers are not watching.

In reality, the teacher did not feel as if it would be possible to ignore the student, since the entire class heard him request the student to move. He tried the ultimatum, and the student still did not move. His classmates began to get worried, because the tension of the standoff made them uncomfortable, and they urged him to comply.

The teacher finally remembered the counterproductivity of the ultimatum approach, and asked the student to remain in the room after the bell rang. When the last student exited the room, the student burst into tears, apologized, and said that he was trying to impress the girl in the next desk and did not feel that he could give in without feeling humiliated.

Preserve the dignity of a student, and you are much more likely to gain that student's cooperation.

LESSON:

Selective Enforcement

A common complaint among students is that some teachers make the mistake of singling out one student for reprimand—or even punishment—when other students are displaying the same inappropriate behavior at the same time. It is best to address disruptive behavior as soon as it occurs with the first student so that you can prevent the behavior from spreading to other students.

Avoid selective enforcement of the rules.

LESSON:

What to Do in the Event of Violence

So far in this book, the overall narrative indicates that the best way to handle misbehavior is with proactive measures that stop it before it begins. Examples of this would be creating an atmosphere of respect and showing the students how to treat others with dignity. Most of the time your students will reflect that behavior back to you and to each other.

Even so, as you emphasize a positive environment, show that you are willing to enforce the simple and reasonable rules of your classroom in an even-handed manner. What happens, though, in the rare cases when all of those preventive actions fail to stop a violent encounter?

IN PRACTICE: You're a first-year teacher assigned to cafeteria duty. One day two boys begin shoving each other, and it is obvious that they are about to start a fistfight. How should you proceed?

1. Pick one of the students and push him to the floor.
2. Push both of the students against the wall with their hands behind their heads.
3. Put your hand on the shoulder of each student and attempt to de-escalate the standoff before the worst of it begins.

As a teacher, you are not a police officer and are not under any obligation to behave like one. At the same time, if you make no effort to stop a fight, you are contributing to your school's failure in its obligation to keep each student safe. What option does that leave?

In any tense situation, your goal as a teacher is to de-escalate the situation.

If you put yourself between the students who are about to fight, experience has shown that in most cases they will stand down out of respect for the teacher. Also, one or both of them is almost always looking for an excuse to avoid or stop the fight without losing their dignity.

If the fight becomes physical beyond your ability to intervene, you do not have to sacrifice your safety. If you are near a phone, call your school's safety office or an administrator, or if that's not possible, have a student do it. Once the fight has been avoided or neutralized, bring each of the students involved to the office so that the situation can be handled according to your school's protocol.

There is no guarantee that this advice will lead to a perfect result in every situation, but sometimes teachers have to choose the least harmful of several potentially bad options, and this approach has been the one with the best outcome most often. One idea, though, always remains true and bears repeating.

In any tense situation, your goal as a teacher is to de-escalate the situation.

Chapter 9

How to Overcome Favoritism

Many students lack basic shelter and food, and survival skills are their priority, not our course material.

—experienced colleague

When teachers play favorites, it's always obvious and very annoying.

—twelfth grader

One of the worst things you can do is to favor the popular kids.

—ninth grader

Being on school property makes my blood pressure rise and puts me in a terrible mood.

—successful twelfth grader

LESSON:

Empathy

Remind yourself that every student in your classroom is facing obstacles that you cannot even imagine. If a student approaches you for help, with schoolwork or anything else, put aside whatever you are doing, within reason, and help the student. The perception that you are unwilling to help can be a powerful cause for resentment for a student as well as his or her parents.

Conversely, showing the willingness to put aside whatever you are doing to help a student goes a long way toward building a positive relationship with your classes, as well as the perception in the community that you are a caring, upstanding professional who is worthy of your position. More importantly, your willingness to help will actually help make you a caring, upstanding professional who is worthy of your position.

Let your room serve as a sanctuary where every student is treated with kindness and respect.

IN PRACTICE: You are a high school teacher in your room during a prep period, and a student runs into the empty classroom, closes the door, and says "I'm really angry—can I please sit in here for just a few minutes?" What is your response, as a teacher, to the student?

1. "Do you have a hall pass?"
2. "Where are you supposed to be? Let's call your teacher. I have work to do."
3. "OK."

When this scenario actually happened to the teacher, the first two responses surely came to mind, and he really did have work to do, but he chose the third option. The world can be harsh, and sometimes teachers have the impulse to want to treat students harshly to prepare them for that world. Experience has shown that life will take care of that on its own. The student who ran into the room felt beaten down and overwhelmed by the stress of a normal school day. The teacher let him gather his composure, then gave him a pass to his next class.

We should make every student feel welcome, because our classroom might be the only place in the world a student feels that way.

LESSON:

Inclusion

For many students, school can be a lonely place. They can feel alienated and ostracized, even as they travel from class to class among a large crowd of their peers. Even students who are part of a group of friends can have the feeling that they are on the edge of banishment, if they make one wrong move or say one wrong word. This uncertainty contributes to the stress every student experiences on a daily basis, and it almost always has a detrimental effect on their ability to concentrate on your curriculum.

IN PRACTICE: You are an elementary teacher, and you notice out your classroom window that a young student is running through a blizzard in the open field next to the school, in a direction away from the building. He is not wearing a coat. Moments later, you see the principal running through the snow in pursuit of the student. What is the most likely explanation for this scenario?

1. The student has no idea where he is or where he is supposed to be.
2. The student wants to play in the snow.
3. The student is so overwhelmed by the stress of an average school day that he felt the need to bolt from the building and run for his life.

Is it possible that the student is clueless? Not likely. Is it possible that he wants to play in the snow? Also not likely, because he didn't take the time to put on a coat before going out in the heavy snowfall. Like many students, he was overwhelmed by administrators, teachers, classes, tests, assignments, bells, and fellow students, all of which not only caused considerable frustration, fear, and confusion to him, but also gave him the impression that he was not wanted at the school, that it is not a place where he belonged or was accepted.

The act of a student bolting from the school building is not an uncommon occurrence, and most schools are equipped to prevent this with cameras, alarms, and school resource officers.

Think deeply about the atmosphere that is created collectively, through all of our classrooms, as students proceed from one to the next, feeling more unwelcome, frustrated, and afraid with each experience, until running from the building into a snowstorm seems like an acceptable alternative to enduring what is inside the building.

Your classroom needs to be the antidote to those feelings of alienation. Avoid language and even subtle reactions that indicate intolerance and bias, and never treat a student as if you would prefer that he or she were not in your presence. Tell the students often that you are happy to see every one of them in your class every day.

Go out of your way to make every student feel accepted, appreciated, and respected for exactly who he or she is.

They may not believe you at first, but if you match your actions to your words, eventually every student in your class will come to believe that you value their presence. The importance of this cannot be overstated, because your room might very well be the only place a student feels welcome and accepted. This will contribute to the goodwill that forms the bonds between your students and you and increases their willingness to give you their cooperation.

Demanding respect only works temporarily—you must earn it by forging a connection with each student, regardless of popularity, and then by showing enthusiasm and expertise when discussing the class and your subject. Let the students feel like you are accomplishing something important together and every single one of them is a part of it.

LESSON:

Appreciation

The difference between honest appreciation and cheap flattery is that honest appreciation is truthful, where flattery is insincere. There is good in every student. It is your job to find it. Make yourself determined to appreciate the individual traits that make each student unique.

The combination of the individual characteristics of the students is what determines the personality of the overall class. Demonstrate to the students that you respect those characteristics by complimenting them whenever possible. The students will pick up on the behavior you model and will treat each other with greater respect. This can sometimes be a slow process, but it definitely pays off eventually. Your class will have a stronger bond, and for some students, it may be the place they feel safest and most appreciated.

Use honest appreciation with each individual student whenever you can.

IN PRACTICE: You are a high school instructor in your first year as a teacher, and you have been given the responsibility of directing the school play because no one else wants to do it. The play calls for a janitor to be revealed as the murderer in a surprise ending, so the casting of that role is especially important. One particular twelfth grader has some of the characteristics that would fit the part perfectly, and he seems eager to take part in the production.

You post the roles granted to each student and minutes later you are met by a group of students and even teachers who say that you

(Cont.)

are making a big mistake assigning a major role to the twelfth grader. Apparently, he had only one line in the previous year's play and almost ruined the entire production through his inability to say the one line correctly. They are all concerned that their play is doomed from the start with him in the leading role. What should you say to the student?

1. I'm sorry—nobody thinks you can do this, so I'm recasting the part.
2. I just discovered a small part that might be better for you!
3. I believe you can do this, so every time I see you, I want you to have the script in your hand to prove you're learning the lines. I know you have it in you!

Once again, it is possible to make a case for any of these three choices. Certainly, the consensus among the cast and crew was that the teacher should choose the first option, and some of the more kind-hearted among them would have been satisfied with the second. Not knowing any better, the teacher chose the third.

At first, it did not seem to be the right decision. The janitor in the play had to quote Shakespeare, and the student had trouble saying the lines even while he was reading directly from the script. The cast was pessimistic. The teacher decided to give praise to the student every time he spoke his line correctly and was sure to offer that praise in front of the other students. Soon, his castmates began to join the teacher in praising him.

The positive reinforcement worked, and on opening night the teacher stood outside the exit doors and heard countless audience members exclaiming their disbelief that our student, cast as the janitor, was onstage quoting Shakespeare so eloquently. One of the common phrases the teacher heard was "I can't believe that was him up there!" When the student graduated, he wrote the teacher a note, saying, "You were the only one who ever believed in me, and I'll remember that until the day I die."

Sadly, that day would be soon—he would lose his life in a car accident a few years later. To this day, the teacher takes some comfort in knowing that the student was inspired to achieve something no one thought he could do, possibly even himself, and suspects the student felt great satisfaction from his achievement.

Do not ever tell students they are not capable of something—tell them they can do it, and make them believe it.

LESSON:

Your Past Comes Back

In one form or another, your past will influence the way you treat students, and it is detrimental to everyone involved, including you. The only solution is for you to recognize that it is actually happening and to do everything in your power to minimize the effects of your biases. No matter who you are or what your experiences were when you were a student, the way that you were treated by different categories of people lives on, buried in your memory, and your lingering resentments manifest themselves in forms that range from subtle to obvious.

As an example, maybe you were an athlete in school, and now that you are a teacher you feel a connection with the athletes who are your students. You feel comfortable around them and form a bond based on stories of past glory in high school sports. Finding something that allows students to relate well to you is a positive thing, at least for those particular students.

The problem is that while you are relating to a certain segment of your students, your remaining students will notice your bond with the few you have chosen and perceive it to mean that you favor one group over the other.

The feeling of being on the wrong end of favoritism is a powerful force that causes frustration and negativity among students, and you need to be sure you never act as if you would rather spend your time with some students rather than others.

Similarly, avoid taking out your past negative experiences with certain segments of the school on your current students now that you have a measure of authority. If you were an average student who perceived that the more academically successful students were looking down on you, you may be inclined to use your newfound authority as a teacher to show the honor students that they are not as smart as they think they are. This is wrong, and you have to recognize when you are doing it and force yourself to stop.

Did you have negative experiences with either gender when you were in school and find yourself being unreasonably harsh toward that group of students now that you have authority over them? Think carefully about that question and answer it honestly to yourself. The same goes for race, religion, socioeconomic status, and any other group of students. No matter which demographic group your students fall under and regardless of your past experiences with those groups, you have a responsibility to reach them.

If you want your students to gain the knowledge, skills, and character that you are attempting to impart, you have to avoid making them feel as if you are holding a grudge against them for reasons they can't comprehend.

What happened to you when you were young is not the fault of your current students, so do not ever take out your resentments and biases on them.

If you find that you can't help yourself despite your best efforts, refer to the section of this book on empathy and remember that each student is fighting battles you cannot imagine. Most students feel as if they are being hit from all directions by responsibilities, pressures, and harsh judgments. All of it can come from families, friends, classmates, and teachers, many of whom you might assume would be on the side of the student.

Chapter 10

How to Utilize Instructional Technology

Multimedia Presentations

Using PowerPoint presentations, video clips, and full movies can be effective practices that contribute to differentiating your approach when used in moderation. Many students will respond favorably when you use technology to bring your material to life with visual excitement. It's important to keep two considerations in mind in order to avoid problems and maximize the effectiveness of these types of presentations.

First, avoid the overuse of both PowerPoint presentations and videos. This is a common mistake, because a teacher can very quickly get comfortable with one procedure and neglect to try others. This is especially true with full movies, which often engage the students' attention with minimal effort on the teacher's part. As with any single procedure, if you use it too often, it can become boring for students and contribute to the perception that you lack the motivation and creativity to use a variety of educational approaches.

Second, be sure that anything you show the students is free from any material that can be considered offensive to a reasonable person. What may be acceptable to one person may be highly objectionable to another. The best way to protect yourself is to get the approval of an administrator before showing a full movie. This will not be necessary forever, but while you are at a vulnerable stage of your career the permission will give you the cover you need to protect your continued employment.

LESSON:

Web Page

Create a website for your students that includes, at minimum, assignments with due dates, topics you will cover each day for the year, instructional videos, links to relevant web content, and any creative methods you can come up with to help students across the spectrum of learning styles.

Another way to use web pages for your benefit is to utilize the review activities on some of the legitimate educational sites. The technology allows every one of your students to stay engaged in the review activities at the same time, so it's especially beneficial for your classes if you seek this type of activity online. Your district will have its own approved sites for you to access, and you can search for activities within those sites.

Technology is best used when it allows all students to engage in an active role while learning the material.

LESSON:

Avoid Potential Problems with Technology

There is no question that technology allows teachers, students, and school systems in general to experience much more productivity and nearly unlimited access to information.

The challenge for teachers is to utilize the technology in a manner that takes advantage of its benefits while minimizing the potential problems brought about by the latest advances in technology.

One potential problem is the increased ability for students to use technology to cheat. They can accomplish this in many ways, but one of them is plagiarism, since computers give students access to many sources, along with copy and paste functions. Of course, students should be formally warned in writing about the consequences of violating academic integrity in accordance with your school's policy.

As always, it's better to prevent a problem from happening instead of punishing students after it happens, and this applies to technology as well.

With that in mind, students need to be taught what actions, specifically, constitute academic dishonesty. Most students don't have a malicious intent, but they often seek out the path of least resistance. Some of them copy and paste information because they consider it the quickest way to achieve task completion without fully understanding that doing so without proper documentation of their sources constitutes plagiarism.

If you have taught them the correct citation of sources, you can still catch any unfortunate student who refuses to heed your warning. The solution, ironically, is to use technology to catch the students who attempt to plagiarize. There are many computer programs available for you to check the honesty of your students' work.

Without naming specific companies or program names, your district has most likely purchased this type of program already, so it would be a good idea to check with your technology coordinator. Again, be sure to inform your students that you are using this program, and they will be much less likely to make a wrong choice when obtaining information from their sources.

Another type of technology problem that is more difficult to catch is when students take the work of another student from a computer, place his or her own name on it, print the assignment, project, or paper, and turn it in as if it is his or her own work. The reason this is difficult to prevent is that the work was usually not published, so it won't show up as being plagiarized from a legitimate source.

There are several possible solutions to this problem, and some of them have the advantage of being preventive. One preventive measure is to have the students work on the assignment during your class time with you closely monitoring the progress of each student throughout the assignment. Another solution is to break your project into small sections at a time, with you checking their work for a completion grade every step of the way.

Sometimes it is difficult to monitor a student's progress if he or she is working on a computer, because even when you break an assignment into small parts, students can share work online. If your problem is this severe, you can take the step of adding the requirement that students write all of their work by hand during class time because you can much more effectively monitor the students' progress and keep them honest. If this seems extreme, it is considerably less trouble than implementing the punishment of one or more students as a consequence of academic dishonesty.

It should be noted that all of these solutions require you to read the students' work thoroughly and with great attention to detail. Many problems can be avoided if students know you are doing that. You can also recognize if one student's writing bears too close a resemblance to another student's work and take appropriate action. Hopefully, your preventive measures will stop these problems before they take place.

Another challenge posed by technology is to teach students that there is a proper time and place to use it. If students are using laptops, chrome books, cell phones, pads, or any other electronic device, it is difficult for the teacher to be sure that they are working on the assignment instead of playing video games, accessing social media, texting, or engaging in any other activities that take their attention away from your class.

The best way to prevent this from happening is to make a rule for your classroom that students can only use electronic devices when you are leading them through a lesson that requires their use. Otherwise, the devices should not be opened or active during your class. This helps the students understand the etiquette concerning the proper time and place to use their computers and phones, which doubles as a character lesson.

If you have a class for which you suspect that this preventive measure is ineffective, you can take a more serious step. A program exists for you to view on your computer everything that is on every one of the student computer screens in your classroom. Once again, your best approach is to consult your technology coordinator about this program. Here as well, hopefully your preventive measures will make this unnecessary.

Use technology to enhance student engagement in your class with your curriculum and minimize its use for distractions.

Chapter 11

How to Handle Your Colleagues

Don't let your mood affect how you act.

—twelfth grader

I think teachers should treat their colleagues with respect.

—twelfth grader

Regardless of your personal feelings, your colleagues carry the same credentials as you; therefore, you should treat them with the same respect that you expect your students to show you.

—veteran teacher

If teachers don't treat each other with respect, it can make students question their credibility.

—twelfth grader

LESSON:

Good-Natured Professionalism

When you meet your colleagues, remember that they may play a role in your life for a very long time. You will want to develop a good working relationship with them based on good-natured professionalism, and the best way to proceed is a two-step process.

Don't be too quick to (1) judge your colleagues harshly or (2) be overly influenced by them.

You will immediately notice practices by your colleagues that you consider philosophically and even ethically suspect, and it is human nature for you to quickly pass judgment on them. Remember that, just like you, they are trying to survive in a challenging profession, attempting to avoid pain and find happiness to the best of their ability.

They, like everyone else, are fighting battles and struggling with aspects of their lives that are not visible on the surface. In addition, they may have reasons for their actions and practices that are also not apparent to you, and they may be finding success with some of those actions.

Avoid as well the other end of the spectrum: don't be overly impressionable when it comes to emulating the practices of your colleagues. Watch and learn as often as possible, but think carefully to decide which ideas will work best with your own personality. Not every procedure works with every teacher.

IN PRACTICE: You are a first-year middle school teacher looking for ideas on how to enforce discipline most effectively, so you observe the class of a veteran teacher. The instructor notices a student who has turned to the student behind him, an action that is disrupting the class. The veteran teacher slams his fist on the student's desk, which causes the student to immediately jump to attention. Later, in your own classroom, you notice a student doing the same thing and are tempted to try the veteran teacher's approach. If you slam your fist on the student's desk, what is most likely to happen?

1. He and his classmates will laugh at your attempt to act tough.
2. He will immediately jump to attention and will think twice before doing it again.
3. He will immediately jump to attention, but your hand will be swollen for a week, leading you to wonder which one of you was really punished.

The first option is a very real possibility, and if it occurs, the teacher will have an especially difficult time gaining the respect of the class. Trying to act tough is dangerous, because it leads to having your students hope for you to fail, and they will take every opportunity to make that happen.

The second option is possible, but the problem is that your reaction will need to become even more extreme during the next incident in order to achieve the same effect on the part of the student. This causes a great deal of negativity, and it is not the way you want to enforce discipline. It may have appeared to work for your colleague, but there were most likely many other factors involved, the most important of which is the connection the veteran teacher developed with his students.

In this case, the young teacher was overly influenced by his colleague. A procedure that worked for the veteran teacher did not work for the new teacher. The student jumped to attention, but began an adversarial relationship with the young teacher that required increasingly extreme methods of discipline. The student forgot about being startled, but the teacher's hand was swollen for a week.

Observe the full spectrum of practices by your colleagues and think carefully about whether any of their methods would work for you.

Cultivate a positive relationship with your colleagues, but stay away from the faculty room unless it's absolutely necessary. The faculty room can be an enticing place: coffee, food, work materials, relaxation, and a chance to become friends with your colleagues. However, faculty rooms are also the place where the most negativity can happen in a school building. In an atmosphere that feels comfortable and private, conversations that may begin with therapeutic commiseration often descend into toxic negativity.

IN PRACTICE: Two ninth-grade students are in the otherwise empty hallway with lavatory passes during class time. As they pass the partially open faculty room door, they hear two veteran teachers discussing, coincidentally, those two particular students who are in the hall. They eavesdrop on the conversation for several minutes and the negativity they hear about themselves is both extreme and of a personal nature, including the prediction of alcoholism and failure based on the parents of the students. What is the most likely response from students under these circumstances?

1. The students laugh about it and refuse to let it bother them.
2. The students knock on the faculty room door and calmly request an explanation.
3. The students are hurt deeply by the personal attacks on themselves and their families and never forget the insult.

In this case, the correct answer is the last one. Three decades after this incident, the former students clearly remember the insult and remain angry and offended by the teachers. They actually bring it up often in conversation. The impulse to share frustration in the supposedly safe confines of the faculty room can allow negativity to escalate and it diminishes all of us. New teachers should remain friendly and professional with their colleagues, but avoid the temptation to spend more time than is absolutely necessary in the faculty room.

The principle of speaking about others with respect also extends to your colleagues. Avoid harsh judgments about your fellow teachers. Just like you, they are battling challenges and adversaries you are not aware of, and they are just trying to survive in a difficult job by minimizing pain, finding occasional happiness, and preserving a shred of dignity.

Do not speak negatively to teachers about other teachers, and above all, never, ever speak negatively about other teachers with your students.

This can sometimes be tempting, especially if your students are comparing you favorably with some of their other teachers, but it is imperative that you avoid that temptation at all times. You can make it a teachable moment and lead by example. If students bring up another teacher in conversation, break in immediately and make it clear that you do not pass judgment on others behind their backs and encourage the students to adopt the same policy.

Be sure to remember this when discussion begins about a student who is not present as well. Whether the topic is a student or a teacher, you can be sure that the students will make that person aware that he or she was a topic of discussion in your class, and it will reflect very poorly on your character. Resolve that you will never allow this to happen.

What if you overhear students saying something negative about another teacher? If it occurs in your class, stop the discussion immediately. Use it as your own learning experience by asking yourself if students might criticize you for the same grievance they have against the other teacher. If they have an objectively reasonable point, remember to avoid the offending behavior or procedure.

What if you overhear students talking about another teacher in a complimentary manner? Again, if it occurs in your class, prevent the discussion from expanding in order to avoid having your colleagues hear that you are discussing them in your room. However, in the case of positive words, you should also take the opportunity to tell the teacher in question that you briefly overheard some very positive accounts from students and be specific about the compliments. It is far better to lift people up than to tear them down, and this sort of exchange can help build a positive relationship with your colleagues. It might also be exactly what that teacher needs to hear on a particularly difficult day.

LESSON:

Professional Courtesy

An important factor in maintaining a positive relationship with your colleagues is to avoid the assumption that your class is more important than theirs. Every one of us believes in the importance of what we teach, but remember that the same belief exists among our colleagues as well. Do not ever keep your class past the bell with the idea that what you are accomplishing with them is too important to confine to your class period.

Every other teacher who is now waiting for those students worked on a lesson plan with a procedure scheduled for a certain number of minutes. If you keep the students after class to finish your lesson, you may be destroying another teacher's lesson. In a related idea, be sure to avoid excessive noise in your room that can cause a distraction to the teachers and students in other classrooms. Your class is not more important than everyone else's—keep that in mind in order to maintain a positive relationship with your colleagues.

Chapter 12

How to Handle Your Administrators

Talk with excitement!

—ninth grader

I think teachers should be respectful toward their administrators, but should also see where the students are coming from with their opinions on school policies.

—twelfth grader

Remember that all of us are fighting battles, just like your students.

—veteran teacher

Teachers should stand up for student concerns with their administrators.

—twelfth grader

LESSON:

Meetings, In-service Days, and Assigned Tasks

Sometimes it is a shock to discover how much time teachers are required by administrators to devote to faculty meetings, in-service presentations, and assigned professional tasks. Experience suggests that it is important for you to resist the temptation to view all of these demands on your time and effort negatively, and to also resist the temptation to voice those frustrations. You will find that staying positive will make you much happier.

Regarding your faculty meetings, you know as a teacher what it is like to stand in front of a group to impart information. How do you feel if the people to whom you are speaking react with passive-aggressive distractions like eye rolls and glances toward the clock? How about more overt disrespect, like mocking, snickering, and pseudohumorous comments and interruptions? You know very well that it is frustrating, if not infuriating. Why would you offer this insult to your administrator? Under most circumstances, presenters can see everything going on with their audience, just like you can see all your students and their reactions to your words.

As a new teacher, your safest bet is to avoid speaking during faculty meetings unless called upon to do so. When that does happen, keep it friendly, good-natured, and positive—just like always. If an argument breaks out during the meeting, keep in mind that nothing gets accomplished that way, unless your goal is to make the meeting last as long as possible.

When many teachers think of in-service days, they unfortunately consider them to be one of two things: a boring waste of their valuable time or a welcome escape from their students. Both of these are negative approaches. The purpose of in-service presentations is to add to your professional development. If you listen carefully and try to apply what you hear to your classes, you will almost always find that you have learned something useful. As a new teacher, you should remember that a short time ago when you were in college, you used to pay for someone offering you this kind of information.

Quite often, faculty meetings and in-service days will include a professional task, usually involving the completion of a project or report analyzing your instructional procedures. Many teachers spend a significant amount of time arguing about the validity and necessity of putting in the time and effort to complete these tasks. In many cases, in the time it takes to complain, you can have the task completed. Even the most seemingly pointless report will require you to think about your instructional techniques from a variety of perspectives you may not have considered otherwise, and you will find that alone to be beneficial.

Faculty meetings, in-service days, and professional tasks have one thing in common: you are going to spend a certain amount of time engaged in them no matter whether you are negative or positive during the process. Giving in to impulses to behave negatively will not only make you less happy during that time, but may also damage your career by diminishing your administrators' impression of your professionalism. Staying positive will allow you to learn something, get better at your job, and give your administrators a positive impression of your professionalism. Which one makes more sense? Either way, you are not getting out any earlier.

LESSON:

More Good-Natured Professionalism

The same principle that you applied to your fellow teachers also applies to administrators, regarding the act of judging harshly and speaking negatively about them. You will have many opportunities to join some of your colleagues in denouncing the policies and actions of your administrators, and it is very important that you resist the temptation. It is easy to overlook the possibility that one of the people to whom you are speaking may inform the administrator of the conversation and implicate you in it. The administrator is, just like you, a human being trying to do the best he or she can in a difficult job.

Similarly, do not judge this teacher too harshly; he or she may not have a malicious intent, but the information is passed to the administrator anyway and it will reflect poorly on your professionalism and character. There are many opportunities for negativity to spread in many directions in ways that are beyond your control, so it is far better to resist the temptation to engage in it altogether. It should almost go without saying, but also be sure to avoid speaking negatively about administrators in front of students.

Cultivate a positive relationship with your administrators, but stay away from the office unless it is absolutely necessary. If an administrator asks how you are doing, respond in a positive and enthusiastic manner. Your administrators should only be used to help you solve problems as a last resort in the most serious of difficulties. If you approach them for help with your day-to-day troubles too often, they may get the impression that you're unable to solve your own problems and that your employment at their school is not progressing well.

LESSON:

Annual Professional Performance Review

Your district will have an agreement with the faculty association about how often an administrator will observe teachers and the criteria and domains by which they will be judged. Familiarize yourself with those criteria and plan carefully for your scheduled observations. Your administrator should inform you about which domains he or she will be specifically evaluating during your observation, and you will need to make sure you reflect those qualities in your lesson.

Some of the observations throughout the year will be unannounced, so it is important that you have a lesson plan every day and that you have your learning targets visible. Learning targets are your objectives for the class that day, written from the perspective of the student, for example, "I can analyze the differences between communism and fascism." You should also have an activity in the back of your mind that you can use if you finish your lesson early during an unannounced observation and you need to fill the remaining time with something meaningful. Remember, student engagement is almost always a quality administrators are looking for when evaluating a teacher's performance.

The evaluations of your individual observations will be combined with other factors such as standardized test scores and evidence of student growth and achievement, based on your district's contract with the faculty association. This will form your Annual Professional Performance Review, or APPR. Take this process seriously, because it will almost completely determine your continuing employment.

Your best approach is to avoid taking the negative points personally and to show an interest in finding ways to improve your performance as a professional. Always thank your evaluator for his or her advice.

You cannot always control how your administrator will choose to perceive your performance, but your positive and constructive reaction to the evaluation and your willingness to accept criticism will go a long way toward demonstrating to your administrator that you are a person he or she would like to continue to work with long into the future.

LESSON:

Disagreements

If you are a relatively new teacher, you may not have reached the stage where you have been granted tenure, if that is even offered in your district. That means that your employment can be terminated with or without cause. Your school can simply decline to offer you a contract for the following school year. If and when you are granted tenure—usually after three to five years of successful performance evaluations—the school will have to follow due process to remove you from your position, but until then, there is nothing you can do about it.

You want to be cooperative, but what if you have a serious disagreement with your administrator during the period before you have received tenure? At this point in your career, within reason, your administrator is always right. If your disagreement is concerning educational theory or philosophy, keep in mind that your administrator has earned the right to implement ideas that he or she believes will be in the best interest of students.

If your administrator wants you to use certain techniques with which you have a fundamental disagreement, be open-minded enough to try the procedure or technique. Also, show your administrator that you are taking his or her advice, because doing so is a demonstration of respect.

You will have a great deal of opportunity to use your own procedures in addition to the ones suggested by your administrator. Someday, you will earn the right to have others follow your example, but in the meantime, have enough humility to try things someone else's way.

What if your administrator asks you to do something unethical? First, be very careful that you are interpreting your administrator's request correctly. If you are certain that he or she has asked you to do something inappropriate or possibly illegal, and a confrontation is necessary, make sure you proceed in a professional manner. Even so, do not be too quick to assume the worst intentions, which is good advice for dealing with everyone else as well.

If you speak to the administrator about the issue, do it in a form where you ask questions and request clarification instead of hurling accusations. Remember, there is a good chance that you have misunderstood, so you should proceed under that assumption.

Later in your career, if you have been granted tenure and have a record of achievement, you will have earned the right to second-guess someone else's philosophy. Even then, do it in a respectful manner, and until then, keep an open mind.

IN PRACTICE: You have recently graduated from a prestigious education program and have landed your first teaching position. You feel that you have been very well prepared with the most cutting-edge pedagogy and educational philosophy and are eager to try out these ideas with your new students. Your principal conducts a professional development workshop requiring all teachers to use a method that your recent education courses have strongly discredited, and he or she points out that your Annual Professional Performance Review will reflect your implementation of this method. What do you do?

1. Have a conversation with the principal during which you use your recent educational insights to point out the flaws in his ideas.
2. Confide in your colleagues about your skepticism of the philosophy.
3. Try the principal's idea and make sure he or she observes you doing so, with the understanding that there is plenty of time to try your own methods.

It is tempting to try the first option, because it is possible to be very sure of your ideas once you have learned them, but assuming that your supervisor is wrong without sufficient evidence shows a lack of humility on the part of the teacher. It's also tempting to choose the second option because you can express your belief in the superiority of your own ideas without the danger of directly insulting your supervisor, but it demonstrates poor character. Also, never underestimate the possibility, even probability, that your words will eventually reach the principal and reflect poorly on your professionalism.

The third option is the right one for several reasons. You may learn something from trying a method you've never used before, and you may also find that it has useful applications that you had never anticipated. Every activity, method, and technique is a tool that is appropriate to achieve certain positive outcomes by reaching some students, and other methods are tools that achieve different advantages with other students.

The field of education is very fad-oriented, where certain methods and terminology are held in high regard, only to be treated with contempt a few short years later and replaced by new methods and terminology. The truth is that all these fads are in some manner useful and achieve positive results with certain students. A balanced approach that uses as many procedures as possible—old and new—is the most effective because you will have the ability to reach the most students.

This scenario can be just as easily turned around, with the levels of experience reversed.

IN PRACTICE: You are a veteran teacher, and a young principal wants to use the cutting-edge philosophies and techniques he has just learned in the course of earning administrative certification. In a professional development workshop, the principal announces that you will be required to demonstrate this method of teaching during his official observation of you. Your success in the Annual Professional Performance Review will be compromised if you do not comply. What is your response?

1. "I have tenure, so I don't care."
2. "Why bother—I've seen fads like this one come and go, and this will be gone soon too."
3. "Why not give it a shot? It might help some of my students, and I'll add it to the different techniques in my rotation."

If you are fortunate enough to teach in a district and state that has tenure, realize that it doesn't mean you're guaranteed a job for life—it just means that your administrators have to follow due process to remove you. You should know that one of the criteria for doing that is insubordination, which can be interpreted as the refusal to follow a direct order. Tenure or no tenure, if your principal wants you to try something, you should do it out of respect, humility, and the possibility that it might work. The first option is wrong.

The second option shows a closed-minded attitude, which is equally as counterproductive when you are dismissing new ideas as when you are doing the same for old ones. Do not become so set in your ways that you refuse to consider the possibility that new ideas can work for you and possibly energize your procedures and reach more students.

The third option is the best approach, because is not only shows deference to the judgment of your principal, but also demonstrates the open-mindedness and flexibility that characterize a true professional.

Different students respond to different methods, so keep an open mind and use as many procedures as you can without arrogance or contempt about any of them, old or new.

Chapter 13

How to Handle
Parents, the Community,
and Public Relations

Never underestimate the power of goodwill.

—award-winning teacher

I like it when I see teachers representing themselves within the community.

—eleventh grader

Teachers should understand the concerns of parents, not avoid them.

—twelfth grader

When it's the school vs. the parents, that's when you know you have a problem.

—twelfth grader

LESSON:

Goodwill

Opportunities to spread goodwill are all around you. Attend as many school events as your schedule allows, such as sports, music, and drama, and take full advantage of your school's open house night to show your enthusiasm for your subject and your students. Parents want to be assured that you care about their children and one way for you to achieve that is through your interaction with them at public events.

Never pass up an opportunity for good public relations.

Spreading positivity and enthusiasm is an investment that you may need to draw on if you encounter a problem. At one particular school, two high school teachers did a "Goodwill Tour" in which they attended every school sport possible and brought the school flag with them. Some of the students participating in sports with traditionally fewer spectators were especially appreciative to know that they had the teachers' support. The importance of all manner of support and goodwill cannot be overemphasized.

LESSON:

Helicopter Parents

Hyperinvolved "helicopter parents" are your friends, not your enemies. Find a way to direct their energy toward a purpose that helps you.

If a parent sends you a message that is a paragraph long and filled with demands for their child, send them a return message twice as long that contains four items:

1. A sincere thank you for their concern and support;
2. Your determination to do whatever is necessary to help their child succeed;
3. An optimistic description of the successes that student has already shown, even if you have to dig deep to find something positive; and
4. An optimistic description of the skills that the student needs to improve, accompanied by the steps you have already taken to improve those skills.

Your message should always conclude with a reiteration of your thanks for their concern and support, as well as your prediction of continued progress for their child. Does this sound like a lot of work? Not compared to the trouble you will endure if you do not get on the positive side of helicopter parents from the start. Remember, you both want the same thing: success for their child. With the exception of rare and extreme parents, staying positive, optimistic, and concerned helps create a good working relationship with them.

LESSON:

Enthusiasm

Open house can induce a great deal of stress among new teachers, but you should be aware that this is your best opportunity to forge a positive relationship with the parents of your students. It's true that, quite often, the parents who show up are the ones whose children are motivated and successful. This doesn't diminish the fact that it is your best opportunity to show parents that you love your subject and are enthusiastic about inspiring their children to love it as well.

Every time you see parents in the community, it is an opportunity to express your enthusiasm for your course and their children. Make it a practice to go to as many extracurricular activities, performances, concerts, and sporting events as your schedule allows. It means a great deal to your students as well as their parents.

The best way to forge a positive relationship with parents is to show enthusiasm for their children and the subject you teach them.

LESSON:

Field Trips

There is no doubt that field trips can be a positive learning experience for your students when you choose your destination carefully. However, you should never lose sight of the fact that your students and their behavior will be visible to the general public, and because of that fact, field trips are very much a form of public relations. If you decide to take your students on a field trip, make sure you have enough chaperones to easily control the behavior of your students.

If you have a high degree of trust that a particular group of students will conduct themselves in a way that promotes the reputation of your school through their good conduct, only then should you consider taking them into public view. If you anticipate any behavior problems with a particular class, it is better to be safe—do not take your challenges with classroom management into a public place to be evaluated by the community.

Teachers can be terminated from their jobs as a result of bad behavior on the part of their students on field trips when it has been reported by members of the public to administrators, who are often very sensitive to public opinion.

If you are within the first several years of your teaching career, it is best for you to avoid field trips altogether, unless ordered by an administrator.

LESSON:

Complaining

Whenever you see members of the community, parents, board members, administrators, or even students outside of school, you need to look at it as an opportunity for positive public relations. Figure out something optimistic to say about your class, your school, and your job in order to build a good rapport with the public. The benefits of this are both mental and practical. In your own mind, you will be better able to recognize and reinforce the positive aspects of your job and will function much more effectively because of it.

In addition, the positivity toward members of the community will make you a more valued member of the staff when cuts are being considered. It will also provide the benefit of the doubt in the minds of administrators, board members, and parents if any trouble should arise. Gratitude for your job is always well received by the community. It is good public relations, and it should be genuine. Of course, there will be aspects of your job that frustrate you. Look for solutions instead of complaining, especially around members of the public.

Never complain about any aspect of your job in front of parents, community members, or students.

LESSON:

Mandated Reporter

An exception to the rule about complaining is when the teacher intervenes on behalf of a student. By law, every teacher is a "mandated reporter," which means that if a teacher has a reasonable suspicion that a student is suffering from abuse, the teacher is required to report it to authorities. You should discuss your suspicion with your school's counselor, psychologist, or sociologist, but ultimately you will need to call the hotline if there is evidence of abuse. Check the listings in your area for the number.

IN PRACTICE: You are a seventh-grade teacher in your first year. One of your students repeatedly disrupts the class by speaking out of turn. You consult your principal, who suggests detention. You threaten the student with staying after school, but the student refuses to show up, so you assign him even more detention, and he refuses to show up for that as well. Your principal suggests that you meet the student outside his last class and escort him to your room, which you complete successfully. The student stays in your room during the detention, then takes the late bus home. For the next several days, the student is out of school. You ask his friends where he is, and they tell you that he can't come to school because he has welts all over his body. When the student gets off the late bus, his father knows he had to stay after school and beats him with a belt buckle. As this student's teacher, what's your next course of action?

1. After consulting with the appropriate school officials, report your reasonable suspicion to Child Protective Services and stop giving detention as a punishment.
2. Consider it none of your business and ignore the situation completely.
3. Tell the student that you're going to force him to stay after school every single time he disrupts your class.

Many teachers would choose the second option, because it's easier to avoid getting involved; however, you are bound by law to report abuse if you are presented with clear evidence. The third option is obviously wrong—and malicious—but was actually suggested to the teacher by a veteran colleague. This is an instructive example as to why you should be very selective about the advice you take from your colleagues. In this case, both the principal and the veteran teacher were wrong. The first choice is correct, and, thankfully, that is exactly what the first year teacher did.

Teachers are mandated reporters, so you are required by law to report reasonable suspicion of child abuse.

Chapter 14

How to Handle Extracurricular Activities and Graduate Work

Be there for your students; don't just be their teacher.

—ninth grader

Extracurricular activities give teachers a chance to connect with their students.

—twelfth grader

Know your subject thoroughly.

—ninth grader

LESSON:

How Many Extracurricular Activities Can You Handle?

You are most likely going to experience pressure to take on extracurricular assignments, such as coaching or advising school clubs. This is a healthy part of the teaching experience because it helps you develop a closer connection with your students. However, you have to be careful, because certain extra-curricular roles can be extremely time-consuming (e.g., coaching) and even controversial (e.g., student council, senior class advisor).

New teachers are often pressured to take the positions that more estab-lished faculty members do not want, and it is important to avoid taking on so much responsibility that it affects your ability to navigate your first years in the classroom. Sometimes the administrator who is offering you the extracurricular position is insistent that you take it, even after you respectfully suggest that you would like to concentrate on the success of your teaching, and may even hint that your continued employment in the school as a teacher is at stake.

In this case, strongly consider taking the position to show your willingness to make sacrifices for the school. A good administrator will not usually do this because he or she knows your priority during your first several years as a teacher is the careful planning and preparation of classes and will want to support your efforts.

Teaching always comes first—it takes priority over extracurricular jobs.

LESSON:

How Much Graduate Work Can You Handle?

Depending on the geographic area in which you are searching for a teaching position, as well as your areas of certification, the openings for jobs may be few and far between. If this is the case, take the opportunity to finish as much graduate work as possible before you accept your first full-time position.

In many states, a master's degree is required to maintain your certification, and if you accept a job before you have completed your education you can expect a good deal of conflicts to arise as you try to figure out the complexities of your first year of teaching along with the rigor of graduate courses. Combine this with the extracurricular activities you will be expected to supervise and you have a very limited amount of time in which you will be expected to master many new and difficult challenges at once.

Finish as much graduate work as possible before your first teaching job.

If you actually achieve your dream job in a competitive market directly following your four-year degree, you can choose to take it, but if you are required to pursue graduate courses, consider taking as many of them as possible during the summer sessions so that they do not distract you from your responsibilities as a teacher.

Do everything possible to avoid distractions and additional demands on your time and attention during your first several years as a teacher.

Chapter 15

How to Overcome Negativity, Avoid Burnout, and Adapt to the Future

If you don't like students, don't become a teacher.

—ninth grader

I don't like it when teachers are too lazy to teach you the correct way.

—eighth grader

I like teachers who have fun.

—tenth grader

No matter how the government tells you to run your class, you can still make it interesting.

—twelfth grader

LESSON:

Shared Unhappiness

Commiserating with your colleagues can be tempting, especially when you are frustrated, but you will ultimately feel better if you stay positive.

All teachers feel frustrated at various times throughout their careers. Often it is tempting to vent this frustration to your colleagues, which in turn prompts your colleagues to describe their own challenges and anger-inducing encounters, all of which results in a great deal of unhappiness all around.

Shared unhappiness builds more of it.

When you're about to complain, stop yourself. Your complaints will most likely fail to change anything, and there is also a good chance that your negativity will be noted and remembered by colleagues you did not realize were listening, as well, and their perception of your professionalism will have been altered for the worse.

How, then, do you deal with frustration and anger?

Stay calm, avoid taking setbacks personally, and look for solutions to problems instead of assigning blame.

LESSON:

Student Reference Letters

One of the most satisfying aspects of the profession of teaching, and one that very few anticipate before entering the field of education, is the act of writing a reference letter for a student. It is also an act that can renew a teacher's faith in the importance of what we do, and there will inevitably be points in any teacher's career where that's necessary. One reason why it is so gratifying is that, among all of the services you provide as a teacher, this one has a direct and practical effect on the immediate future of your students.

Many of the effects teachers have on students are delayed, or at least are not immediately visible. The knowledge, skills, and character a teacher helps build within a student are not always apparent, but a reference that helps a student win a scholarship, job, or place in a college or university has a dramatic and tangible result in the student's favor.

What if you feel that the student who asks you for a reference letter is not deserving of your recommendation? Think very carefully before you decline to provide a reference for a student, and you should definitely avoid writing a negative one. It is also not necessary for you to distort the truth by claiming positive traits that don't exist. Instead, look for the good qualities that actually do exist. Everyone has them, and it is important that you get into the habit of finding those positive attributes in every student, or it will be very difficult, if not impossible, for you to build a connection with your students.

Confine your remarks on the recommendation to the good qualities in the student and expand on them to create a detailed letter. It is helpful if you ask the student for a list of activities, sports, clubs, and honors he or she has accomplished, and your guidance department can usually help with that. The list allows you to add detail to your letter so that you can back up the positive comments you write about the student, making the reference letter considerably stronger and more effective.

An example of the structure of a good reference letter is to begin with a description of who you are and your connection with the student, the courses you have taught him or her, and a description of that student's academic performance in your classes. The next section can describe the extracurricular activities, sports, and leadership positions demonstrated by the student. Your description carries more weight if you describe activities you have actually witnessed the student performing.

You should also include a section on character. This section, as well as the others, has more power if you relate examples of situations in which the student demonstrated the good qualities you're describing. Finish with a reiteration of your recommendation for that student based on the attributes you've mentioned and a prediction of future success for that student. There will always be a deadline for the submission of recommendation letters, so take great care to be sure you are completing and submitting it on time. Keep in mind that a lot is at stake for the student.

The recommendations we provide for students can create opportunities for them that will dramatically affect the rest of their lives in a positive manner, and it is a reminder to the teacher that our profession is one in which we are privileged to take part.

LESSON:

Review Your Procedures

The best way to keep yourself and your class fresh and interesting is to constantly review your own procedures. Keep the ones that have an obviously positive reception by students where you can see an improvement in motivation and understanding. Remove the procedures that seem to be boring the students because they are less likely to learn that way. That leaves room for experimentation.

LESSON:

Learn from Your Students

One of the most effective ways to avoid burnout is to recognize the uniqueness of each new combination of students you have in your class every school year. You can gain a great deal from engaging with those students to find out about their interests. Of course, it's important to be sure you're devoting an appropriate amount of time to making sure you're adequately covering the curriculum to maximize student mastery of the knowledge and skills necessary for their success. However, in the process of doing so it is inevitable that there will be down time, such as when the class has finished a test or assignment with a few minutes left before the end of the class.

Rather than waste those minutes, you should take advantage of them by asking your students about their activities and interests. When a student begins discussing an interest about which you have very little knowledge, take the opportunity to learn about it. Ask the student to elaborate about his or her interest by asking questions.

Do not be afraid to show your lack of knowledge about a subject not associated with school because it will give the student a sense of pride and help build a connection that will increase the student's motivation. For your part, you are getting to know your students on a deeper level, which helps you guide their instruction more effectively. As a bonus, it helps you learn about subjects you've never learned about in the past, as well as helping you to avoid burnout through a better connection with your students.

LESSON:

New Courses

In most school districts, teachers can request their preference for the courses and grade levels they will be teaching, with administrators making the final decision. Sometimes, however, your administrators may require you to teach a course or grade level in which you have little or no experience or interest.

The reasons for this can be logistical in the sense that your school's staffing, combined with the programs and courses your school is intent on offering, may necessitate some faculty members having to teach courses outside of their preference, experience, or even their certification. It is true that it is in the school's best interest to honor your preferences because of your interest, knowledge, and expertise, but sometimes that is not possible. When you are assigned courses outside of your preference, embrace the opportunity rather than complaining about it.

Teaching new courses and grade levels forces you to think about your procedures from a fresh perspective, and you will find that many aspects of the new assignment will help you grow as a professional. The changes you will need to make with different courses and grade levels will keep your outlook fresh, which in turn will help you prevent burnout.

Embrace the opportunity to teach new courses and grade levels.

LESSON:

Cross-Curricular Collaboration

Another step you can take to avoid burnout is to collaborate with teachers in other subjects—who also have your students in class—in order to form projects that include the curriculum for all of your courses. For example, if you are a tenth-grade English teacher covering Renaissance literature, collaborate with a tenth-grade world history teacher whose course includes Renaissance history, and an art teacher who can cover Renaissance painting and sculpture in order to create a project for the students that helps them learn all those subjects. If a presentation is involved, you may even want to include credit for a public speaking or speech class.

As with all project-based assignments, make sure that the time and effort you and your students devote to the activity has enough value in terms of the knowledge and skills gained by the students. This is especially important for your goal of covering all of the material in your curriculum and for your students mastering the state standards in your course.

Cross-curricular collaboration helps students see the connections between subjects as well as the relevance of your material and helps the teachers view their material with a new perspective.

LESSON:

New Ideas

Quite often, learning from your students can occur in a context that allows you to gain a new educational procedure from the experience. If students make suggestions on activities that would help them learn the material, don't dismiss those ideas without carefully considering each one. If the procedure is unfamiliar to you, it does not automatically mean that the idea is defective. Students know which activities allow them to become engaged in the learning process, and at least some of their ideas will produce that engagement.

IN PRACTICE: A seventh-grade teacher near the end of her career explains a review activity to her class that she has used for many years. A student respectfully suggests that they use a review activity from a reputable educational company that is found on the internet, and the other students enthusiastically agree. How should the teacher proceed?

1. "Thank you anyway, kids, but I've been doing this for a long time, and I know the best way to review."
2. "Thank you for the suggestion. I'll look it up to see if it's legitimate and maybe we can try it together in a few weeks."
3. "Let's look it up together, and you can show me how it works."

The first option is a safe one, especially considering the fact that the teacher has many years of experience successfully using her review activities. It is unsettling to consider that the students might know something that you do not, especially with regard to the professional practices within your career.

However, if you react in this manner, you will not only lose the opportunity to discover a new activity that the students obviously feel is engaging and productive, but you have also shown that you have very little regard for their judgment. This can be frustrating for students, especially if they have good reason to believe they are right in their judgment.

The second choice is also safe, because you will be giving yourself the opportunity to investigate the activity to not only be sure it is productive, but also to be sure nothing about it is inappropriate. As mentioned earlier: it is not a good idea to show a video that you have not previewed. In this scenario, though, the suggested activity is with a reputable educational company. Unfortunately, however, if you deny your students the act of showing you the idea they have in mind, you will once again lose the opportunity to validate the students' expertise and strengthen your bond with them. You will also lose the energy of the moment, as well as a potentially valuable review activity.

Since the online procedure is with a reputable educational company, the teacher chose the third option, and asked the students to show her immediately how the activity works. Following a tutorial by many excited seventh graders, it turned out to be the most engaging educational review procedure the teacher had ever experienced. She reports that she continues to use the procedure to this day.

Try new ideas that will inspire and motivate your classes, because new and exciting techniques will inspire and motivate you along with your students.

LESSON:

Forgive Yourself and Others

Teaching is a high-profile position. Depending on your class sizes as well as your longevity, you may encounter four thousand individuals during the course of your career. You will live on into the future in their memories, and you will do your best to make your influence a positive one. However, in the course of dealing with that many people, sometimes under stressful conditions during formative times in their lives, you will make mistakes. Those mistakes will begin on your first day and continue every day throughout your career.

Sometimes you will get away with an error in judgment, and other times you may have consequences with your administrators and others because of that error. Do not let your mistakes demoralize you to the point where you leave the profession. Remember that you will spend your career helping thousands of students, and the world will be better for it. Your mistakes do not even begin to counteract the positive effect you will have on many individuals as you help them unlock the future that lies ahead for every one of them.

You need to forgive yourself for missteps, minimize the damage, apologize and make restitution, learn from the experience, then move forward.

There will also exist people who have been hurt or inconvenienced by you in some way, possibly without you being aware of it or understanding the reason, who at some point display their hostility and resentment toward you. You need to also remind yourself that another person's negativity toward you may have nothing to do with your actions, but instead with someone else who has in some way caused pain or stress in the person's life.

In other instances, you may have unwittingly served as an obstacle to the goals of some of your students, colleagues, and administrators, and they may have taken action against you. Sometimes their negative actions are the result of an effort to achieve their aspirations, and other times they are the result of weakness, insecurity, and defensiveness. What all of these cases have in common is that they are best handled in the same manner: forgiveness on your part.

If you want to avoid burnout and gain the most satisfaction possible from your career, you need to forgive yourself, those who have held your mistakes against you, and those who have acted against your interests with or without apparent cause. They, like you, are doing their best to survive and are often demoralized by forces and events that you cannot see.

Throughout your career, you will face many challenges and setbacks. Through gratitude, humility, sincerity, forgiveness, and magnanimity, you can continue to gain satisfaction throughout your career from serving as a positive role model for many students. In the process, you will help them achieve the knowledge, skills, and character that will serve them long into the future.

Author's Note

In this book, my students and I have offered advice on how to deal with some of the practical challenges you will face as you begin your teaching career. An effective way to avoid mistakes is to learn as often as possible from both the positive and negative experiences of others. For example, here is an event that had a lasting effect on me, and I would like to pass it along because I found it to be instructive.

IN PRACTICE: A male teacher addresses his fifth-grade classroom with the question, "Does the room seem brighter to you?" to which a student replies, "Maybe the sun is bouncing off your bald head!" Rather than laughing, which the offending student is desperately hoping for, the class collectively gasps in surprise and discomfort. What is the teacher's response?

1. "Why did you say that? Answer me! I do not appreciate your disrespectful comment, and I'll be taking this up with your parents as well as the principal. Now gather your belongings and go to the office!"
2. "Please see me after class, and we'll have a talk."
3. After a pause, "Ha ha, good one—you're probably right!"

I think it is possible to make a case for all three of these options. The first one demonstrates that the teacher refuses to allow disrespect and upholds a high standard of conduct, but also reveals the teacher to take himself or herself so seriously that the other students will begin to root for the offending student. This is not the way for a teacher to own the room. The second choice seems reasonable and allows the student to save face, but still punishes the student and upholds a high standard of conduct. That seems fair.

Here's a confession: this encounter actually happened, and I was there. However, in this scenario I was the student, not the teacher. It was 1975, I was in fifth grade and trying out different personalities, like many ten-year-olds do. On that day, I thought maybe being the class clown would be a way to earn a positive response from my classmates.

Here is what my teacher actually did: during the long pause where the class gasped and I winced in fear and instant regret, my teacher looked at me and decided that I needed a break. He sized me up as a decent kid who was just trying to gain acceptance, so he chose the third option. I was so grateful to my teacher that I never again said a disrespectful word to him.

Of course, if the student continues to show disrespect because he or she now believes it is possible to get away with it, the teacher should move on to the second choice. In my experience, the first option never produces a positive result, and, believe me, I have tried it. One more thing: the original incident happened in 1975, and I remember the encounter word for word. That is a long time to remember something that clearly, and it is a testament to the power a teacher has to make an impression on a student that lasts a lifetime. Later I encountered that wise and merciful teacher as an adult and I reminded him of the event and expressed my gratitude.

I paid his kindness forward a quarter century later when, as a teacher, I responded the same way to a student making a similar comment to me. Remember the scenario I described in the introduction section? I was standing in front of a group of ninth graders as a relatively new teacher. I introduced an educational activity for the class by saying, "You know what I haven't tried in a while?" to which a student replied, "A sit-up?"

In that moment I remembered my fifth-grade teacher and quoted him almost verbatim. My response was, "Good one. You really got me there!" I gave him a fist bump for added measure. As I recall, he was never disrespectful toward me again. The distant memory of my fifth-grade teacher's wisdom became a guiding principle for the manner in which I treat my students.

I would like my closing message to you, however, to be a suggestion to keep all of this in perspective and to remember what is genuinely important. I have learned what I consider the most wide-ranging and significant lesson from one particular event.

Early in my career, I attended the retirement party for a respected teaching colleague. Throughout the final years of his career, I watched as he navigated the difficult balancing act of dealing with his colleagues, parents, administrators, and board members. His retirement party included a unique feature: students from each decade of his career stood before the guests and shared personal stories of how my colleague affected their lives.

This was an instructive moment for me. I realized that many of the frustrations that cause stress on a daily basis in the teaching profession are less important than the attention we give them. Instead, what lives on is the relationship we have with each individual student. The speakers that night did not know anything about the details of what went on behind the scenes with their teacher. They only remembered the example he set as a distinguished, respectable, and decent human being, and it inspired them to reach for a higher standard in their own lives.

No matter what frustrations you encounter as you begin the process of becoming an effective teacher—and there will be many—do not ever forget the honor it is to play that role in the lives of your students. Make sure they know every day that you are aware of this privilege. The connection you make with each of your students and their memory of your positive influence, above all else, will be what lives on into the future.

Best wishes for a successful career. I genuinely hope you find as much happiness and fulfillment as I have experienced in this wonderful profession.

Jeff Julian
March 2015

Appendix A

Suggested Motivational and Review Activities

PIZZA CONTEST

Offer to bring homemade pizza (if food is allowed in classrooms in your district) to any class that has a perfect rate of assignment completion. That means every student has to complete every assignment, every day, on time and up to an acceptable level of quality all the way until the conclusion of the marking period (or the entire year, if you prefer) in order to win the pizza. Important note: check for student food allergies and bring a backup treat for students who are unable to eat the pizza. The contest also works if you substitute an entirely different food for the pizza, as long as it provides motivation for the majority of the class.

It is a good idea to show large pictures of the homemade pizza on your screen throughout the quarter. This is one instance where peer pressure can have a positive effect, because just one student completing an assignment even one day late can ruin it for the entire class.

Character Points (in conjunction with the pizza contest)

In order to reinforce positive behavior, whenever you see a student doing something courteous, kind, or considerate for another student, announce that action to the class and tell them that the student has just earned character points for their entire section. Keep an informal tally in your memory, and at the end of the quarter, if more than one class has a perfect record of assignment completion, pizza is served to the classes in the order of their character points.

It is much more effective to reward good behavior than to punish bad behavior.

HOOP OF KNOWLEDGE REVIEW GAME

Attach a small basketball hoop to the wall in your classroom, making sure it is in a location that is visible to all of the students but away from their seating so that the area around the hoop is unobstructed. Split the class into two teams according to their seating, in order to minimize the disruption of students moving around the room. Flip a coin to determine which team will go first. Ask a question from the material on your upcoming test to the first student seated on the team that won the coin toss.

If the student answers correctly, he or she can proceed with a foam basketball to the hoop and take a shot from behind a predetermined line for an extra point (or select a designated shooter), which will be added to the point the student earned for his or her team by answering correctly. If the student makes the shot, that team retains possession, and the next question is asked to the next student in line on that team. If a student gets the question wrong, or misses the shot, possession goes to the other team. Be sure to allow any student who obviously doesn't know the answer to pass the question to the other team immediately without undue attention or humiliation.

You can add to the excitement by setting an alarm on your phone, after which all point values are doubled or tripled. In order to keep the game running smoothly, teams can lose points for cheating, complaining, or unsportsmanlike conduct. At the end of class, the team with the most points wins.

TRIPLE THREAT REVIEW GAME

Split the class into teams of three. Again, if you do it by the seating that is already established, it minimizes disruption. Ask a question from the material on your upcoming test to the first group (in the order of seating), and allow that group ten seconds to confer with each other, at which time they will give an official answer to the question. If they are correct, they win a point for their team, and the next question will go to the group who is next according to the order of seating.

Whether the group answering the question gets it right or wrong, the possession still moves on to the next team in the order of seating. Again, be sure to let a team pass the possession to the next team quickly if they do not know the answer, in order to minimize embarrassment. In order to add to the excitement, set an alarm on your phone to sound often during the game, which calls for a "free for all" question.

After you ask the question and say "go," the team that shouts out the answer first gets a point, and the possession proceeds from there in the order of seating. Again, in order to keep the game running smoothly, teams can lose points for cheating, complaining, or unsportsmanlike conduct, as well as, in this case, excessive and extraneous noise when shouting out answers. At the end of class, the team with the most points wins.

FULL-CLASS CHALLENGE

This activity tests students' ability to work together to make a complex inference, which in this case is to consolidate information to create an educated guess and to build a correct answer out of confusing and vague shreds of misleading clues. Pick a captain for the entire class. Choose a small, obscure detail from your course material that students cannot retrieve from their memory.

Present the question to the class. Collectively, the class has one question of their choice that they are allowed to ask the teacher, plus one additional clue of the teacher's choice, and three guesses. All requests for questions, clues, and official answers are presented by the captain, who represents the efforts of the entire class. Ideally, clues as well as answers to the students' questions should be as confusing as possible, forcing students to think deeply and strategically.

In order to add excitement, when the captain gives the final answer, tell the students that their time is up and the last answer is final. Then choose a quiet, withdrawn member of the class to have veto power over everything that has been decided. That student will be able to let the class's final answer ride or replace it with an answer of his or her own. If the class successfully wins the challenge, they can receive credit for a question in their written assignment as a reward.

You can alter the helpfulness and specificity of your clues in order to either lead the class to the correct answer or alternately to make the process more challenging with convoluted information. Either way, the teacher orchestrates an activity that reinforces the ability of students to make intelligent and strategic inferences and to process information using higher-level thinking skills.

SCRAMBLE CHALLENGE

In this contest, students compete individually to answer a difficult, obscure question from the material covered in class. The specific question should be challenging enough that students should not be able to easily recall the answer. The teacher asks the question, says "go," and the first student who correctly answers the question wins. Here's the catch: as soon as a student verbalizes an incorrect answer, he or she is eliminated.

Since the first correct answer wins, the students have competing incentives to both answer quickly and to hold back, especially if you offer clues in order to bring the game to a conclusion. A single scramble challenge shouldn't last more than a minute. If it approaches that time, make your clues more helpful until you lead the remaining students to the correct answer.

THE CAGE OF DESTINY

Students can learn a great deal from the act of individually conveying information to the entire class, and the prospect of doing so can serve as an incentive to complete an assignment or take notes on a section of reading in a thorough and detailed manner. Purchase a small bingo wheel and assign each student to a number on one of the balls. The student whose number is chosen is required to make the presentation to the class. If you spin the wheel directly before the presentation, every student will have to be sure he or she has a detailed knowledge of the content in order to make an impression of competence to the class, since most students will want to avoid embarrassment.

There are several ways to add to the intensity and drama of the selection process. The teacher can choose the numbers one at a time for the students who will not have to speak, leaving the last remaining number as the student who will make the presentation. This reverse drawing only takes a few minutes extra, but adds a great deal of excitement to the process.

Students can also avoid reacting about whose number was chosen throughout the spinning of the wheel so that the speaker is revealed at the conclusion of the drawing. Another variation has students standing for the drawing and only sitting when each student's number is called. It is also effective to have the students remain standing until all numbers have been called, then have the students whose numbers were called all be seated at once, revealing the student who remains standing as the one responsible for making the presentation.

In addition, the teacher can allow the winning student to invoke the "Coin of Redemption," where if the winning student wins a coin toss, he or she can pass on the responsibility of making the presentation to the student attached to the previous number drawn.

Adding even more to the competitive spirit of the game, the teacher can keep a tally of how many times each student has been chosen throughout the year to make presentations. The winner can be awarded the "Cage of Destiny Trophy" at the year-end academic awards ceremony in order to reward their efforts in making presentations to the class, and students who were never chosen can receive the "Avoidance of Responsibility Certificate." Both awards are significantly sought after by students.

Appendix B

Quick Reference

The following are the main points we covered in this handbook:

- It is a tremendous privilege for you to stand in front of a group of young people and presume to explain to them what the world is like.
- Always remember the honor of playing this role in the lives of your students and make sure you give an indication to them every day that you remember it.
- You are likely to be happier and more productive if you focus on your students and refuse to engage in controversies about the public's view of the profession.
- The factor that makes teachers important is the role they play in the lives of their students, not the act of telling others about their importance.
- Stay positive in the face of criticism by showing gratitude and humility.
- Your salary, benefits, and conditions should not be deciding factors in whether or not you will pursue a career in education. The main consideration is whether you want to play an important role in the lives of students. If you go into teaching for the summer vacations, you will find that it is a long way to the summer.
- Make sure your students know that the reason you are a teacher is because you like working with them and want to help them.
- As teachers, our influence extends beyond what we even know.
- If you are going to pursue a teaching position in another area or state, research the details carefully before you go.
- Make sure you have multiple copies of your diplomas, certificates, reference letters, and any other supporting documentation you will need. Keep all of your background information compiled and stored in one easily accessible location for when you are filling out applications.

- Read a book outside of school, and think about what it teaches you about life.
- When asked about your background in the subject material, always concentrate on expressing what you know, not what you do not know.
- Be sure to show a deep interest in the subject matter in the course for which you are interviewing and a desire to help the students discover the same fascination with it that you have.
- You should be sure to have several stories ready to convey to your interviewers, each involving optimism, overcoming obstacles, and student success.
- If you combine the approach of optimism and enthusiasm while keeping in mind the qualities that represent you at your best, it is difficult for you to go too far wrong in your answer to any question.
- During your interview, above all else, stay positive and enthusiastic at all times. Remember why you love your subject and why you love working with students, and then convey that to your interviewers.
- Throughout the interview process, make sure that any mention of students is optimistic and hopeful.
- You should enroll in the union if it is offered in your district in order to help maintain a reasonable balance between administration and teachers, but avoid public displays of protest until your position is more secure.
- The atmosphere you create, including your physical surroundings and your demeanor, will be reflected back to you by your students.
- The tone of the classroom is the responsibility of the teacher, not the students.
- Within reason, teachers need to display their own unique practices and expectations in order to serve the needs of all students.
- Create and maintain a positive relationship with your school's secretarial, technical, and custodial staff members. They will play a large role in your life.
- Never assume that you outrank anyone, and be sure you never behave as if you think you do.
- Before the start of the school year, map out the time frame for each topic throughout the year so that you are sure you will be able to cover the entire curriculum with your students.
- As always, the teacher's own conduct is the most effective character lesson of all. When you react to adversity with integrity and honor, students notice and are influenced positively by it.
- You should have a lesson plan with, at minimum, objectives, procedures, and the state standards covered for every class, every day.
- Use your district's online technology to keep parents and students informed about their progress throughout the year.
- Take the time to read student assignments, score their tests, and post their grades with as little turnaround time as possible.

- Own the room! A good way to establish that the room will follow your positive, optimistic example is to greet your students at the door.
- Show the students that you like spending your time with them in your classroom. Never give them an indication you would rather be somewhere else.
- Your students will be significantly more motivated to follow the rules of your school as well as the ones you create for your classroom if you are conspicuously following them yourself.
- Making yourself available to help students will significantly contribute to your reputation for professionalism. Put aside personal tasks, within reason, to place student assistance as a priority.
- Always review and explain the rationale for the rules of your classroom with your students.
- Personal and medical issues can play a role in a student's requests for the restroom, nurse, or water fountain, and challenging a student on this issue when the student has legitimate cause for the request can result in permanent harm to your credibility with the student.
- Establish and follow the rules, but keep the process as positive as possible.
- The idea of a self-fulfilling prophecy really exists. Give the students a vision of themselves that they want to live up to.
- Bullying is a problem that deserves the attention it has been getting, and we need to do everything in our power to stop it. There are a lot of things that happen between students when adults are not watching.
- Be cognizant of the impression you are making on your students. They look up to you, and your words and actions are powerful.
- There is a reason why you chose to be a teacher of the subject you are teaching—it is because you love the material. Make sure the students see why you love it.
- All students, from the highest achieving to the least motivated, crave intellectual stimulation. If they do not get it from you and your lesson, they will be tempted to get it by disrupting and undermining you and your lesson.
- In the course of explaining complex concepts to students, make the information relatable to their lives.
- Do not be afraid to use your own talents and interests to increase the interest and understanding of your students.
- Your time with the students is precious; never give them the impression that you are willing to waste that time with excessive distractions and pointless tangents.
- One method of discussion involves the teacher posing an "essential question," which is fundamentally important to the main idea of your topic. Ideally, your question should be inquiry based, which is to say that it calls for the higher-level thinking skills of analysis, synthesis, and evaluation.

- It is all right for you to serve as a source for the knowledge and comprehension bases for the students to build on in a discussion, but avoid going overboard. Keep in mind—it's about them, not you.
- The job of a teacher is to teach students how to think, not to think for them.
- Encourage your students to form their own opinions based on facts and their own logic, values, and experiences. Remain objective and avoid bias at all times.
- Keep all the levels of thinking and learning in mind as you plan your lessons, and create a balance where students are using the information in your curriculum for higher-level activities.
- Your approach to any topic should be a balance between discovery, student-based approaches, and explanatory, teacher-based discussions to serve the entire spectrum of learning styles.
- Group projects can be an effective way for students to become engaged in the learning process and utilize skills that they normally would not use in an academic class to further their learning of your subject.
- Your first goal—and most important task—as a public speaker is to gain the goodwill of your audience.
- If you make a mistake, admit it without hesitation and move on.
- Take care to avoid bias in your language against classes, races, genders, orientations, or any other group of people.
- Some of your students are going to become our carpenters, bricklayers, electricians, plumbers, and mechanics. They should never be made to feel as if the validity and importance of their skills are in any way minimized by you or others in the class.
- You are responsible for the education of all students who have been placed in your classroom, regardless of any potential challenges they bring with them.
- Your instructional strategies should include provisions for the entire spectrum of learners, including those with special needs who are entitled to accommodations; gifted students who are desperate for a challenging, rigorous approach; students who are learning English for the first time; and everyone in between. As you plan each one of your lessons, do not ever neglect to think deeply about this.
- Never use public humiliation against a student.
- It is far better to help your students understand your course material before you give them the test, rather than reprimanding them if they fail to perform well on the test.
- Never express anger, frustration, or impatience at students for their lack of knowledge or ability—that lack of knowledge and ability is your responsibility to fix, and it is the reason you have a job.
- Stop cheating before it begins.

- Never give up hope for any student, and never let any student lose the prospect of success.
- The most effective teachers include relevant thought processes, skills, test formats, and curriculum that help students prepare for standardized tests. They balance these with other worthy educational practices like creative projects, discussions, discovery-based assignments, and evaluative papers in which students take and defend a position.
- Some things are more important than school.
- Try to avoid adding to the misery of your students and lift them up instead.
- We all want acceptance, appreciation, and respect. The best way to achieve that is to forge connections with others based on goodwill.
- Keep your voice calm.
- Preventing disorder before it begins is preferable to dealing with problems after they happen, and every problem you avoid makes your classroom a better place.
- Your demeanor should strike a balance between kindness and authority.
- When unforeseen things take place, the laughter is going to happen. It can be behind your back, at you, or with you. It is always better to laugh with your students.
- Sincerity wins every encounter.
- Every minute with your students is important, so do not give them the impression that any of that time can be discarded.
- Never give an ultimatum to your students.
- Disruptive behavior should be handled calmly through direct conversation with the student, away from the view of the rest of the class.
- Preserve the dignity of a student, and you are much more likely to gain that student's cooperation.
- Avoid selective enforcement of the rules.
- In any tense situation, your goal as a teacher is to de-escalate the situation.
- Let your room serve as a sanctuary where every student is treated with kindness and respect.
- We should make every student feel welcome, because our classroom might be the only place in the world a student feels that way.
- Think deeply about the atmosphere that is created collectively, through all of our classrooms, as students proceed from one to the next, feeling more unwelcome, frustrated, and afraid with each experience, until bolting from the building into a snowstorm seems like an acceptable alternative to enduring what is inside the building.
- Go out of your way to make every student feel accepted, appreciated, and respected for exactly who he or she is.
- Demanding respect only works temporarily—you must earn it by forging a connection with each student, regardless of popularity, and to then show

enthusiasm and expertise when discussing the class and your subject. Let the students feel like you are accomplishing something important together and every single one of them is a part of it.

- Use honest appreciation with each individual student whenever you can.
- Never tell students they are not capable of something—tell them they can do it, and make them believe it.
- The feeling of being on the wrong end of favoritism is a powerful force that causes frustration and negativity among students, and you need to be sure you never act as if you would rather spend your time with some students rather than others.
- What happened to you when you were young is not the fault of your current students, so do not ever take out your resentments and biases on them.
- Technology is best used when it allows all students to engage in an active role while learning the material.
- The challenge for teachers is to utilize the technology in a manner that takes advantage of its benefits while minimizing the potential problems brought about by the latest advances in technology.
- As always, it is better to prevent a problem from happening instead of punishing students after it happens, and this applies to technology as well.
- Use technology to enhance student engagement in your class with your curriculum and to minimize its use for distractions.
- Do not be too quick to judge your colleagues harshly or to be overly influenced by them.
- Observe the full spectrum of practices by your colleagues and think carefully about whether any of their methods would work for you.
- Do not speak negatively to teachers about other teachers, and above all, never, ever speak negatively about other teachers with your students.
- You cannot always control how your administrator will choose to perceive your performance, but your positive and constructive reaction to the evaluation and your willingness to accept criticism will go a long way toward demonstrating to your administrator that you are a person he or she would like to continue to work with long into the future.
- Later in your career, if you have been granted tenure and have a record of achievement, you will have earned the right to second-guess someone else's philosophy. Even then, do it in a respectful manner, and until then, keep an open mind.
- Different students respond to different methods, so keep an open mind and use as many procedures as you can without arrogance or contempt about any of them, old or new.
- Never pass up an opportunity for good public relations.
- Hyperinvolved "helicopter parents" are your friends, not your enemies. Find a way to direct their energy toward a purpose that helps you.

- The best way to forge a positive relationship with parents is to show enthusiasm for their children and the subject you teach them.
- Teachers are mandated reporters, so you are required by law to report reasonable suspicion of child abuse.
- Teaching always comes first—it takes priority over extracurricular jobs.
- Never complain about any aspect of your job in front of parents, community members, or students.
- Finish as much graduate work as possible before your first teaching job.
- Do everything possible to avoid distractions and additional demands on your time and attention during your first several years as a teacher.
- Commiserating with your colleagues can be tempting, especially when you're frustrated, but you will ultimately feel better if you stay positive.
- Shared unhappiness builds more of it.
- Stay calm, avoid taking setbacks personally, and look for solutions to problems instead of assigning blame.
- The recommendations we provide for students can create opportunities for them that will dramatically affect the rest of their lives in a positive manner, and it is a reminder to the teacher that our profession is one in which we are privileged to take part.
- Embrace the opportunity to teach new courses and grade levels.
- Cross-curricular collaboration helps students see the connections between subjects as well as the relevance of your material and helps the teachers view their material with a new perspective.
- Try new ideas that will inspire and motivate your classes, because new and exciting techniques will inspire and motivate you along with your students.
- You need to forgive yourself for missteps, minimize the damage, apologize and make restitution, learn from the experience, then move forward.
- If you want to avoid burnout and gain the most satisfaction possible from your career, you need to forgive yourself, those who have held your mistakes against you, and those who have acted against your interests with or without apparent cause. They, like you, are doing their best to survive and are often demoralized by forces and events that you cannot see.
- It is much more effective to reward good behavior than to punish bad behavior.